This Perverse Generation

To
My Mother

Unless the Lord build the house~

they labor in vain that build it.

This
Perverse Generation

by Carol Jackson Robinson

Catholic Authors Press
Hartford, Connecticut

Contents

Chapters 1 to 11 of this book are reprinted
from *The Torch*

·1·

False Foundations

IT PLEASES ME that the Communists keep nipping at the vulnerable spots of what was once Christendom; outraging us now by an atrocity, now by a major theft. It shows that God has not abandoned us to our complacency.

I am happy about strikes, too. They are like the hiccups, lately more like the retchings, of a body which declines to digest poison. Strikes are all that prevent our settling down to undiluted avarice as a way of life. With everybody now avaricious it is natural that there should be recurrent quarrels over the spoils. We should be grateful that they prevent our suffocating from a surfeit of materialistic comforts. The thing most to be dreaded about our schemes which do not include God is that they should succeed.

I rejoice that the United Nations cannot achieve harmony on the basis of expediency, and I wait for them to show some slight concern for objective righteousness or the common good; some faint thirsting after justice. It seems so obvious, as the Holy Father has said, that therein, and therein alone, lies hope of peace.

I like to see people fail in the advertising business; maybe God is reaching for them. The fluctuations of the stock exchange affect me in inverse ratio to their effect on brokers. I knew of a broker once who lost his fortune and found his soul.

The domestic infelicity of those married after being several times divorced neither surprises nor pains me.

We have built our world on phony foundations. God gave us a site and laid down the proper foundations for society. Instead of building our houses as indicated, we wandered into nearby marshes and sand dunes, and tried to construct there. We built a lot of houses, but they are springing leaks all over the place. We keep propping them up here, bailing out the basements there, redecorating further on. All to no avail. They threaten increasingly to collapse.

"Let's go back to the original site and start over again. Maybe the houses there would be more sturdy," someone suggests.

"Yes, we probably should have built there in the first place, but it's too late now. We've invested so much money in our houses that are built upon sand, that obviously we can only continue to pour good money after bad. Surely the Architect won't mind. We'll put a picture of him in our bedrooms and implore him to send us more props."

The Architect does mind. He always heaps blessings on men. What if in our time the blessings come in packages marked "war," "bankruptcy," "nervous breakdown," "broken heart," "failure," "frustration." Shall we not still praise Him and, chastened, return to the original site to help build Our Father's House?

Everything fails ultimately if it is not of God. It fails not because God sends a destroying angel, but because a perverted use of a natural thing sets in motion its own internal laws to bring revenge. God is not tormenting us. He is only allowing us to suffer some of the natural consequences of our disregard of Him. He is letting us discover that the double-feature-super-de-luxe-everything-electric-night-clubbish ideal we almost touched was a mirage; in the hope that we shall presently see that it was also a nightmare.

The moral disorders in the world are of several sorts. We

tend to stress the *subjective* element in sin as being the only criterion in moral disorders, forgetting, too often, the *objective* evil itself. Birth control is an objectively grave sin in itself, even if all the women of the nation practice it in good conscience. All the women might conceivably go to Heaven; the nation is going to collapse.

There are certain ways we have to use our bodies and our minds. There are certain basic considerations in the organization of society. These all constitute the natural law, which is written not so much in books as in nature. You find out what it is by observation and by reason, and not necessarily through revelation (although revelation reinforces our knowledge). You will find abundant reference to the natural law in St. Thomas Aquinas. The whole of Catholic philosophy and moral teaching is bound up with it.

Interestingly enough, the Catholic Church alone upholds the validity of the natural law today. We sometimes hear that "all men of good will" can collaborate on the basis of the natural law, because it is binding on all of them. Binding or not, it is not recognized very widely outside the Church. Neither Luther nor Calvin really believed in the natural law, nor do most Protestants today. Reinhold Niebuhr, a leading Protestant theologian, attributes the difference between Protestantism and Catholicism in regard to the natural law to the fact that the Catholic Church has more confidence in the power of reason than does Protestantism. We should recognize that most Protestants do not honor the natural law. It helps explain their support of birth control and euthanasia.

Reinhold Niebuhr is right. It is a matter of confidence in human reason, and wherever there is a violation of the natural law by a Catholic in good faith, you can be pretty sure his trouble is ignorance or intellectual sloth. The mess in the world today is largely in consequence of widespread perversion of the natural law, as much from ignorance of it as from anything else.

Too much emphasis in contemporary Catholicism is on good will and not enough on good understanding, for good will is not held in a vacuum, and ignorance is often culpably sinful. If all Catholics have a moral duty to understand their faith at their level of secular education few of us are going to be saved. A college graduate, for instance, ought to have a pretty good understanding of St. Thomas and of the natural law. He ought to see the major issues involved in restoring society to God. Do you, by any chance, think he does?

Pius XI said in another connection: *"In our day and age, unenlightened heroism is not enough."* How much longer are we Catholics going to pretend that if our hearts are in the right place we can safely continue to live in an intellectual void?

We cannot say it often enough: *it is the root things that are wrong in our society*, and that usually means a perversion of the natural order some place. What good does it do to distribute books and magazines to hospital patients if the books and magazines are no good? How can you be conscientious in a stupid job? How can you perform the duties of your state in life if you have no state in life? How can you have a really Christian family life in a New York tenement? How can you have a liturgical life on a purely commercial farm? How can you have a community life if you have no basis of unity?

Our job is not to superimpose piety on a distorted foundation; our job is to go back to the old foundations and build anew. As long as we continue to throw good money after bad we shall hasten the day of collapse, and stand as a barrier to a world hungry for the true Church: for we shall have nothing to offer the starving world but some social scheme warmed over and diluted from the Communist camp.

·2·

The Atrophy of the Parish

St. anne's is imaginary. It is more or less representative of the average city parish in America. A brief view of it will demonstrate how circumstances foreign to the Church have affected, to the point of atrophy, this basic ecclesiastical unit.

St. Anne's is now some seventy-five years old, its parishioners drawn largely from second- and third-generation Irish, thoroughly Americanized.

In Western Europe the parish has always until now been the unit of community life, the center around which towns and villages grew. It often continued to be the geographical measure of temporal activities after its spiritual authority was disregarded. It has been otherwise in America, where cities grew around a factory, or a harbor or a railroad junction, with the churches incidental to the growth of the neighborhood. The Catholic parish church did not even begin as the *center* of the community; now it is on the periphery of such desultory community life as exists. St. Anne's parish is measured in city blocks, so many east and west, so many north and south. It is not coterminous with the postal zone, it is not coterminous with the political ward. It measures nothing except itself, and that arbitrarily.

5

If St. Anne's Church is not the center of the territory in the middle of which it stands, what is? Nothing. The local people gather in the A. & P. Supermarket, the movie house and the bars, but these are not centers either. There is no center because there is no community, there is merely an agglomeration of people living closely together, yet impersonally. There is no reciprocal relationship between them. Even their work is outside the territory. They could form a community if there were a very strong unifying force, but it would have to be very strong indeed, because all the natural forces militate against an organic relationship between them.

THE BOND OF THE HOLY EUCHARIST

The practicing Catholics in the territory embraced by St. Anne's parish constitute one-fifth of the population. Nearly as many again are fallen-away or desultory Catholics, while another fifth is Protestant and Jewish. The remaining two-fifths disregard religion. Let us return to the one-fifth who practice the Catholic Faith. They can be seen streaming in and out of the church on Sundays, a large number of them communicants.

Many are the ties that bind men: common racial background, common work, family connections, the bond of suffering, shared cultural tastes. All these are as nothing compared to the oneness of men who partake of the Body of Christ. A man is more closely bound to a stranger at the Communion rail than he is to his own wife or mother in the natural order. What is curious about St. Anne's then, and all the parishes like it, is that the unity which does in fact exist among the parishioners hardly flows into action at all. The most real community in the world does not proceed to realize itself. While everywhere men are forming groups and desperately looking for a common bond, those who have a common bond sufficiently strong to overcome all natural differences refuse to form groups and carry out all the implications of their unity. They are not even conscious of their oneness, and emerge from the church to seek some other, natural, basis on which to associate with their fellows.

THE LITURGY AT ST. ANNE'S

You have never been in St. Anne's but you could guess what it looks like. There is a statue of Our Lady over one side altar; of St. Joseph over the other. Somewhere, prominently, is a statue of the Little Flower. Why should the tastes of the local parishioners be any more distinctive in their devotions than in their daily life? Everyone listens to Jack Benny, reads "The Egg and I," goes to see "It's a Wonderful Life," markets at the A. & P., and makes novenas to St. Theresa. It is the American way of life. The Catholic is the universal church, by which up until now it was not meant that the non-essential details of worship were everywhere the same, but that the inexhaustible richness of Christ's Life found expression in a marvelous variety of external forms according to the temperament and genius of local groups.

Novenas are the big attraction at St. Anne's. They are in the language of the people, not only because they are in English, but because they have *emotional* appeal, for people who live in a world which has descended to the level of feeling. They also give people a chance to participate by singing hymns, which are maudlin in their sentimentality, but popular. The trouble with the emotional approach, from a practical point of view, is that you have to keep increasing the dose, as with dope. The advantage of the Mass, besides its being Christ's sacrifice, is that the Life received in the Holy Eucharist grows richer and richer of Itself. It is the blaze from which we could so easily all catch fire.

Liturgical reforms have begun to touch St. Anne's. The nuns try to teach the children Gregorian chant, with some success.

No attempt has yet been made to get the mute congregation actually to participate in the worship.

The clergy at St. Anne's do a marvelous job of dispensing the sacraments. Masses are offered at convenient times, and punctually. Altar linens are immaculate. Sick calls are very promptly attended to. All parish records are kept efficiently. The weakest point is the Sacrament of Penance. Here again service, efficiency and knowledge are present, but so much more, not strictly in the line of duty, is needed. Many a parishioner is seeking from 'irreligious psychiatrists help on problems essentially spiritual.

FINANCING ST. ANNE'S

It cost a lot to build St. Anne's Church—about seven times the actual construction expenses. Building was made possible by a bank mortgage which over a period of many years and several depressions sucked up a vast tribute from the parishioners, predominantly poor maidservants. Maybe it would have been better 'just to have given the churches to the banks. It certainly would have been better, if possible, to have built them with the voluntary labor of the parishioners. But that is all water under the bridge now. St. Anne's has paid off the mortgage and seen the last (we hope) of the usurers. What if four generations of pastors had to make themselves more into money raisers than spiritual shepherds? Maybe Father So-and-so will get a chance now to attend primarily to the spiritual well-being of the parish. And maybe in time the memory of bingo and benefits will fade. Maybe a spiritual renaissance will provoke the parishioners to contribute gladly and lavishly for thankfulness that they have Christ with them, for the love of God and the knowledge of their solemn duty to support the church. Maybe then names will not have to be published to shame those who are remiss and it may even happen that the collection of a seat tax at the door will have become just an unpleasant memory.

SEPARATION OF CLERGY AND LAITY

The priests at St. Anne's live almost in isolation from the parishioners. This is primarily because many of their normal functions have atrophied, as we shall show. Since there is no real community, there is no opportunity for the clergy to enter into the life of the community. They remain on the periphery of life, engaged almost solely in work connected with the administration of the sacraments and of parish affairs.

There is no anti-clericalism at St. Anne's, nor is there any basis for it. The clergy do not live in unnecessary splendor, nor do they regulate unduly the temporal affairs of their parishioners. The one possible source of friction on the economic level has not to do with luxury but with security. Priests and religious in our day enjoy an enviable freedom from the haunting fear of insecurity which plagues the proletariat. Whereas we should, on the whole, rejoice that this is so, nevertheless it is not healthy for religious life that secular life should fall below it in material advantage.

There is a certain clericalism in St. Anne's parish, perhaps a remnant of the near worship of the clergy by the persecuted Irish. When the Sodality meets, the young women are favored with an inspirational talk by the curate, during which their only responsibility is to show a polite deference. So it is with all the parish societies. They are run by the priests; meekly attended by a handful of docile and pious souls, who (possibly in consequence) are not given to thinking for themselves. It is enough for them to know that Father Such-and-such says it is all right to do so and so.

Unfortunately, Father Such-and-such is not in a very good position to discover the real problems of his parishioners. He cannot, like the Curé of Ars, go about the offices and factories, watch men at their work and in their businesses; so later to confound them from the pulpit. He has not fathomed the complexities of modern economic and social problems; nor will he be able to do so without lay help. This is where Catholic Action should come in, as a bridge, and an informative avenue, between the clergy and the modern world from which they are shut off. But it is hard to start Catholic Action at St. Anne's, and part of the reason is the residual clericalism, that certain reluctance of the priests to give real initiative to the laity. The last study group died aborning, despite its excellent membership and Father's forceful leadership. At the time there didn't seem very many important things to consider.

ST. ANNE'S AND THE APOSTOLATE

Theoretically the pastor of St. Anne's has all the souls within the parish borders under his shepherding care, though his responsibility toward different groups varies. Theoretically the parish should give evidence of its Divine Life by a constant ferment among the local unbelievers and a stream of converts. The amount of "dead life" in the parish is painfully obvious even to the casual observer, and it was very depressingly revealed by the last parish census. But what is to be done about it? The apostolic work of the Church is in the hands of foreign missionaries and a few national figures such as Msgr. Sheen. Even supposing a parish priest had the time for such work, it is not easy to win converts today by ringing doorbells. Even among such prominent characters as the local storekeepers, there are many who have fallen away from the Church and are never asked to come back; there are many unbelievers who could be persuaded to turn to God if someone bothered to persuade them. Catholic Action would help provide a bridge for conversions. The Legion of Mary would go after the strayed in a way which has proved successful.

ST. ANNE'S AND CHARITY

Of all the functions which the parish has lost, none is so crippling as that of dispensing charity. If the rich of the parish helped the poor of the parish; if the well of the parish helped the sick of the parish; if the idle of the parish helped the over-burdened of the parish, through the intermediary of the parish priest; if the parish had a soup kitchen, or a bread line or a clothing distribution center or a house of hospitality, there would be visible evidence of the Divine Life in it. As things are now, charity is channeled through diocesan bureaus, or governmental agencies, which are too big and too impersonal to stimulate community feeling. But charity belongs on a personal basis and should be centered in the parish church. To channel it elsewhere has about the same effect on parish life as each member's eating out, and in a different restaurant, would have on family life.

ST. ANNE'S AND SOCIAL LIFE

It must not be supposed that St. Anne's is unaware of its social ineffectiveness. It knows all about mounting divorce rates, birth control, and juvenile delinquency. But since it has been pushed out of public life and stripped of most of its functions, there doesn't seem much to do. You cannot mold a people in five minutes a week on Sunday. You have to attract them somehow to the church. The answer which St. Anne's is acting on is recreation.

Social life is a legitimate function of the parish. It originally was, and should still be, an overflow of the joy of being a Christian. It should be primarily a celebration of Holy Days, in a fitting manner, close to the liturgy. The attempted destruction of Catholicism in our world did its most thorough work here, especially in the English-speaking world. Holy Days were

B

suppressed and were finally replaced by patriotic holidays. The Puritans, who even tried to do away with Christmas, frowned on dancing and general merry-making. As recreation was gradually restored under the pressure of human nature, it was a transformed recreation. Formerly it had centered around the parish church, now it is commercially centered around the local Times Square. Formerly there had been processions; now there is an occasional parade. Formerly it had been a family affair, now there is a strict separation of parents and children. Formerly it was religious, now it is secular. Instead of gay, colorful, graceful, innocent and community folk dances, we are now visited with modern, paired-off, graceless, ballroom dancing done to erotic music (with anything but innocent words) under circumstances conducive to impurity. Formerly there were athletic contests, strictly amateur and generally participated in. Now we have spectator sports, professionalized and subject to racketeering control.

When St. Anne's undertook seriously to center recreation around the church it did not make any effort to restore organic recreation, rooted in the liturgy, but more or less undertook to subsidize secular entertainment. They got a juke box, hired swing bands for fortnightly dances, and outfitted the altar boys in baseball clothes so they could participate in the diocesan league contests.

Clearly there has been a mistake somewhere. Thoughtful parents are now sending their children off to strict schools so as not to subject them to the immoral influences of dances held, whether in parish halls or local hotels, under the auspices of the clergy. Priests are themselves distraught over the conditions prevailing.

Meanwhile, by a curious coincidence, the Communists have taken over the folk dancing which the Church has despised and which was yet so much its heritage. In New York City they have hired, and consistently filled, huge halls with young enthusiastic people whom they gradually attract to The Party in this way. This unsophisticated group recreation tends of its nature to create fraternal spirit and enthusiasm.

PARISH AND FAMILY

The basic unit of the Church is the parish. The basic unit of society is the family. Parishes should be made up of families, but St. Anne's operates in many respects as though it were catering to the individual. In this regard it is following the erroneous pattern of modern economics.

All the parish societies at St. Anne's tend to separate families. Father goes to the Holy Name, Mother to the Altar Society, while the children are distributed among the sodalities, confraternities and scout troops. If each member of the family loyally attended meetings there would be scarcely any opportunity for real home life. Even at Mass the family is not together. There are obvious advantages to a children's Mass, but the fact remains that it is one more separation of the family in a day when families can scarcely survive the sundry disintegrating factors.

THE COMING REVOLUTION

There is a revolution taking place in the world today. Whether bloody as abroad, or bloodless as here, it is turning life upside down and establishing the future on new foundations. If St. Anne's parish is going to be a dynamic unit in forging the new world for Christ, it too will have to change drastically. The question to ask is not "Is there anything wrong in what we are doing?" but "What can we do to be effective in a changing world?" It is not a matter of whether church societies are well run or abundant, but a matter of whether or not they are suited to the times.

The relationship of its parishioners to St. Anne's is of a sort suitable to a former age. It harks back to the times of

Catholic poverty, Catholic persecution, Catholic ignorance
even, in the midst of a triumphantly rationalistic, secular,
Protestant world. About the year 1900 the holy life of the
Catholic Church was the hidden life of the Catholic Church.
While learned and rich men denied and ignored God, Mother
Cabrini was busy in her obscurity among despised immigrants,
and nuns nobody ever heard of quietly made their oblation of
reparation for the sins of mankind. It was an age of reparation
and of preparation. The lay American Catholic didn't have a
chance of orienting the temporal order to Christ. Heroism for
him was in keeping the faith. In such a situation the Church
wisely chose to keep the laity as close as possible to herself.
The societies for laity were devotional, concerned with the
increase in personal piety. The watchword was "Don't make a
mixed marriage," because the Church saw that, when Catholics got mixed up with non-Catholics, the Catholics usually
capitulated. The whole policy was one of retrenchment and
withdrawal, with emphasis on piety and reparation.

Things happen fast these days. Almost overnight the post-
Christian world has become bankrupt, chaotic, and despairing,
necessitating a reversal of policy on the part of the Church. We
are now in an era of intense apostolicity rather than reparation. The laity are not now the least members of the Church
who participate in a small degree in the higher life of the
priests and religious. The laity are the front-line troops of the
restoration of the social order to the Church and the priests
and religious have an increasing obligation to form the laity
in a manner suitable to the times. One of the things that is
necessary is a whole set of new forms, new lay organizations
attached to St. Anne's. The new organizations have to be
suited to the contemporary situation. Specialized Catholic
Action is one of them, the Legion of Mary is another, and
there is room for many more which will grow up with the
times. They all have certain principles in common which derive from the nature of the modern lay apostolate. The men-

tion of a few of these principles will show the radical nature
of the change that is necessary.

1. A new relationship of priest and laity is involved. The
laity have to have a certain *initiative*. Because they have to
deal directly with the temporal situation, they have to make
their own observations and use their own prudence, subject
to the Church's teaching and control. The priests, in relin-
quishing the initiative, keep the control, usually through
acting as chaplains rather than as chairmen. At meetings of
Specialized Catholic Action groups, for instance, it is
customary for the priest to remain entirely silent, but he
meets during the week with the leader and actually has the
confidence and the control of his group much more strongly
than does the usual priest in charge of, say, the Holy Name
Society. And Specialized Catholic Action is officially under
hierarchical direction and control.

2. The old-type organization, in an effort to reach *as many
parishioners* as possible, customarily dilutes the dose of
Christianity to a pretty low level, and often introduces social
life and athletics as the chief feature of meetings. The new
organizations work on the entirely different principle of
leadership, giving much time and intensive training to a
handful of leaders, and counting on them to infuse life into
the whole parish. It is better to have one saint than five
hundred lukewarm but practicing Catholics. Of course, a
pastor is responsible for all his parishioners and must try
to lift the general level of Catholicity, but the emphasis is
changing. It is better to give *time* to the formation of a few
than to try, against the currents of history, to inspire the
multitude to effective action.

3. There is a return to basic principles and high spirituality.
It is not inspiration that the modern lay apostle needs, so
much as basic knowledge and deep spirituality. Novenas
and non-theological sermons are mostly on the inspirational
level, and the old-time church organization was equipped
to handle real problems but not basic ones. Today a lay
apostle has to aim at the highest spirituality, such as was

formerly thought suitable for cloistered religious. He needs good spiritual direction and a technique of operating that will help develop that spirituality. He also needs real principles and a priest chaplain who knows his St. Thomas and his social encyclicals.

St. Anne's cannot but change in the next few years, for the revolution is beating at its doors, by means of a succession of laity who want something *more*, and, negatively, in the more and more drastic nature of its problems. There does not seem to be any rest for the Catholic Church. There does not even seem to be an interval of rest and satisfaction to be allowed those valiant and self-sacrificing Catholics, and especially priests, who built churches and convents and schools and hospitals from one end of this vast country to another, and who educated their poor immigrant parishioners until now Catholic laity are in positions of influence in every secular field. One would think that enough, but it isn't. There is a world to be won for Christ and now it is the apostolicity of the Church that must be re-learned.

·3·

The Elimination of the Human Element

God (FOOLISHLY AS MODERNS SEEM TO THINK) entrusted His visible creation, and indeed His Incarnate Self, to that unpredictable, inexact, capricious, fallen and sinful species known as human beings. According to *His* plan, everything is to depend upon how perfect men are, how good men are and how docile men are to the grace which will make it possible for them to run the universe and work out their salvations (two not unrelated tasks). One useful way to view contemporary society is as a gigantic effort to circumvent this arrangement of God's, as a refusal to be dependent on the capricious personal factor, as an attempt to eliminate the human element. Evidences of this plot are everywhere. They range from the "untouched by human hands" boast to the "Don't let your relatives remember that they had to pay for your funeral" warning. In this America, home of the rugged individualist, and founded, more or less, on the right of private judgment (errors both), personality and individuality have alike given way to standardization and economic mechanization.

Observe the phenomenon of the Gallup Poll. Its basic assumption is that Americans are so stereotyped (with variations in the rubber stamp according to income and locale) that a very small sampling of public opinion will accurately reflect the actual ratios which would obtain if the entire population were queried. The Gallup Poll is the reverse side of the coin of mass circulations and coast-to-coast networks. We respond to set stimuli in set fashion, not unlike the law of averages in coin tossing; not unlike the reflexes of guinea pigs. A Gallup Poll could never have worked in, say, France of fifty years ago. Its accuracy is not so much the measure of Dr. Gallup's genius as of our degradation.

Now that the Gallup Poll has been defeated in the 1948 election (to the delight of everyone) we may be spared further developments of the principle on which it was operated. The Gallup Poll has been pre-testing movies for guaranteed financially successful plots, and was trying to find a method for determining pre-publication sales of books. None of the learned men who learnedly investigated the failure of the election polls has had the simplicity to suggest that men have free will and therefore can *never* be reduced to formula, so they have not learned their lesson. However, the general public, having shown this extraordinary power of limited self-determination, may remember to laugh instead of admire.

THE CLOAK OF ANONYMITY

When a man wants to fire someone he ought not to fire, he takes refuge in an intermediary. Most men cannot bring themselves to do *personally* what they cause to be done anonymously. That is why the business tycoon often seems an enigmatic figure. He will display great personal affection and charity toward his valet, while callously (and impersonally) ruining his valet's brother through manipulations of stock. He will almost invariably be kind to his secretary and office boy, whom he daily sees, while quite possibly being ruthless toward the 5,000 employees he has not personally met.

Similarly with money lending. We would be horrified if a

college classmate, a neighbor or a fellow-parishioner, were to charge us interest on $100 borrowed for our wife's confinement. But we take it for granted that the bank will not trust us, that it will demand collateral, and that, having secured the loan against any conceivable loss of the principal, it will then charge us interest. Technically, according to the laws of nature and the Church, this is *usury* and reprehensible. The practice of it came about for various reasons, but it was made possible by *depersonalizing* the transaction. Investments involve similar injustices which the anonymity of the stock exchange makes possible.

THE ATROPHY OF THE PERSON IN INDUSTRIALISM

Nothing is so striking about the machine age as the fact that we have perfected machinery instead of men. The typewriter is a very clever little machine. But is the typist clever? Apart from the dexterity of her fingers, she is, on the average, as unaccomplished a maiden as the world has ever produced. If you asked her what her talents are, she wouldn't know what you were talking about.

The radio is ingenious too, and no doubt taxed the ingenuity of a handful of scientists. So is the printing press, the automobile, the airplane, the telephone switchboard. These, and all our other gadgets and machines, now practically run themselves. We are very pleased with ourselves because of this perfection we have wrought in *matter*. We fail to reflect that, for one thing, we are playing right into the hands of tyranny. Bombing planes don't *quite* operate by themselves. Someone has to decide where they will go to drop their bombs. All we have done is to make it possible for a single tyrant, in control of our material perfection, to tyrannize millions of us. This is just the dictator angle of a situation which has a number of other angles. One Hollywood writer can set us all weeping, one banker in a key position on the Board of Directors of Pyramided Corporations can decide who will eat breakfast tomorrow and what his food will be. It's what we get for neglecting to be about what we should have been about—the perfection of man, not matter. If we had perfected men instead of machines, it would be impossible for a dictator to take us over. He would not be able to confuse us by his specious reasoning, because our intelligences would be alert, disciplined, and accustomed to independent judgment in the light of known principles. He would not be able to bribe us, because we would have moral strength, disciplined against temptation by the practice of mortification. He would not be able to intimidate us, because each man would spontaneously resist injustice and brutality, with no thought for his own safety; it would be impressed on his very nature that honor is preferable to life with dishonor, that it would be better to die, for instance, than to countenance (as did recently the citizens of Vienna) the bold, broad-daylight abduction of two girls from a cafe for the purpose of their violation. This is just one more of thousands upon thousands of such incidents which add to our shame. Isn't it obvious that the Hitlers and Stalins of our day could never succeed in a better moral climate, in a world where men have clear Christian ideas and strong moral sensibilities, where individual men are splendid, and never mind about "progress"?

Labor-saving devices mark the atrophy of the human being. The major way we reach perfection (in the natural order) is through work, and modern men have robbed us of work, substituting instead organized monotony. Work tests our mettle, develops and matures us, teaches patience, taxes our minds and our ingenuity, helps us to understand the Creator because we are co-creators. Why do we shudder at the thought of returning to a craft civilization? A craftsman is molded and strengthened and perfected. He is *something* and *somebody*. A woman is made more perfect in spinning. Is she made more perfect in a trip to Macy's and back on the subway? It does something to a woman to make bread, it only *tires* her to go and buy bread in the store. So now we have finely tempered steel—but adolescent men and women; we have visual education—but undisciplined minds; we have iron ships—but wooden men. We are like a man playing a player piano, who has fewer and fewer (and less and less pleasing) tunes, who might have become a pianist, and might even have become a composer.

LABOR UNIONS AND PATERNALISM

Not content with material machinery, we are setting up human machinery to eliminate personal relationships among men. From the point of view we have chosen, it is interesting to observe labor unions. These aggregations of men should have worked for an ultimate moral goal, but they chose to remain within a materialistic framework. They should have tried to perfect their members and to persuade their employers to a more Christian view; but they chose to use physical coercion. They should have tried to unite and harmonize; instead they chose to emphasize differences and start class warfare. They are determinedly *impersonal*; they want nothing to do with charity, but only with justice and coercion. So really the situation gets farther and farther from solution. The J. O. C. in Belgium is an interesting contrast to the unions. It *did* concentrate on the perfection of *men*, starting with the workers, and within ten years had employers and employees in the factory in which they began gathered together "as one in Christ to discuss their mutual problems," and from this flowed material benefits all around, far in excess of what materialistic unions have yet achieved.

There are places in the South where there is a notable absence of racial tension, despite grievous discriminatory practices. In the North there are all-white factories, with good washrooms and excellent wages, which are pervaded with the tension of class antagonism. The difference in the two situations is the human element. In the Southern situation there are, as very many people will testify, countless instances of personal kindness, charity and trust, which make for harmony and peace even in a framework which is undemocratic, if you like, and in many ways very unjust (charity covers a multitude of sins). It is better to have a paternalism in which virtues can flow, than social security, just wages, legal equality and tiled bathrooms where everything is regulated by impersonal contract instead of personal contact. When will we believe that love is the only thing that will make the world work? When will we discover that charity really is the oil of society, and that Christ's teachings are not arbitrary, but rather the instructions by which alone we shall live?

THE IMPERSONALITY OF PERSONNEL

The art of understanding and reading men is among the highest arts. It comes from knowing God, understanding the purpose of life, having oneself suffered and prayed, and being a formed, mature, moral and spiritual person.

The modern personnel man is a colorless figure on the lookout for machine parts. He doesn't take into account the human factor any more than is necessary. The last thing he's looking for is a "character," or a saint, or even anyone with an independent mind. Note how he operates. To cover up his own inadequacies, and to mechanize the process as much as possible, he makes use of an ever-increasing number of psychological tests, he tries to read the man by a series of clues given by what is measurable in man. Man is essentially spiritual, and spiritual things cannot be measured, so it all is really an elaborate pretense. There is one company I know of (there are probably many) which puts prospective employees through a series of tests taking several days. They prefer this to interviewing because it "saves time." Whose time? Certainly not the prospective employees' time.

Now, once a person is employed, he is expected to be as inhuman as possible. He's not to say what he thinks, or use his brain outside of strictly prescribed channels, or discuss religion, or show charity to the man at the next desk, or show concern over the salvation of anyone's soul. He cannot be a human being. But he can be an animal. It is, in a way, the worst of all indictments of the industrial-capitalist system, that a man noticeably concerned over the salvation of souls would be fired, whereas fornication and adultery (since they do not threaten the system and sometimes keep the workers happy) are generally countenanced, and often indirectly encouraged.

DE-PERSONALIZING THE PROFESSIONS

It is a conspicuous and depressing fact that the calibre of professional men and women is declining, while the material elements, such as efficiency systems, medicines, instruments, etc., are (ostensibly) improving.

Take doctors. It used to be that medical training and practice all tended to perfect the medical man, who, especially after a number of years in general practice, acquired an almost uncanny facility in diagnosis. He acquired a keen sensitivity to physical ills and could discern them, and treat them, with great skill. The diagnostician has become obsolete. The good doctor now is the young doctor, because he is up on the latest medical discoveries. It is not because *he* is something wonderful, but because the medicines are potent and the operating equipment of the finest, and he's read up on them. In medical centers there are not diagnosticians, just corps of specialists. You have to have tests and x-rays, and weights and measurements, and that somehow adds up, so that a decision as to your ailment can be made almost mathematically. There is no reason to suppose that the decision is any more accurate (it is probably less so) than the old general practitioner's

diagnosis. It is certainly more expensive, and this is partly due
to the cumbersome method, but also in part to a yearning for
penthouses and yachts on the part of doctors, because they
lack the joy of personal power and achievement and need
something to assuage their discontent.

Teachers are another standardized product of the day. Obviously teachers should be great men and women, exceptionally
well-developed *persons*. If they were, you could trust them to
teach more or less as they pleased. But we have turned our
attention away from what the teachers are, from their own
moral calibre and wisdom as human beings, to what they
know (factually) and especially to an unnecessarily detailed
analysis of the technique of teaching. We try to perfect the
syllabus, not the teacher. We have undermined the dignity of
the whole profession. And the teachers, not having been themselves perfected, and having practically no personal responsibility about what or how they teach, are restless too. So they
are led, by the blind who lead us, to suppose that more money
will somehow soothe them. But it is a spiritual and personal
problem, and money will not solve it.

The social worker is one more of an endless number of ex-
amples of the same thing. Among the curious tasks of social
workers is that of teaching women the things women always
knew by instinct, except that the social worker's advice is not
usually as good as the instinct was. With the assistance of Freud
and the social work schools we now learn that a first child
tends to be jealous of a new arrival in the family. What mother
in history (until now) has not known as much? And isn't it
silly for social workers to try to teach Italian peasant women
dietetics?

THE OIL OF CHARITY

Babies in orphan asylums die without affection, even if all
their physical needs are supplied regularly, scientifically and

hygienically. If we were to succeed in eliminating the personal element entirely, society would just die, that's all. The only reason we manage to limp on as things are is because charity does continue to flow despite the conspiracy to eliminate it. We owe what stability remains in society to the despised, contraband personal element.

Take the case of an enormous business company, for instance. If you question the corps of file clerks or machine operators, you will find their main concern is not the remote purpose (whatever it is) for which the company exists. Nor are they held in captivity by an intense desire further to line the pockets of the corporation executives. To some extent they are held by their own greed, but the overwhelming reason that they find their lives tolerable and that they continue to behave as robots, is because they like the other girls, because they are concerned about Marjorie's coming marriage, or Joan's sick mother. There exists, because of the humanity of petty clerks, a sort of community life, by virtue of which alone our system continues.

So it is all the way down the line. Organized, impersonal charity only works at all because of the personal trust, interest and kindness of some social workers. Medicine stands up because of the real compassion and self-sacrifice still to be found among doctors. Even party politics survives because of the human element and personal consideration on the part of the ward representatives of a Tammany Hall.

KILL THE GOOSE

We, in our folly, deplore rather than exult in the very factor that makes things work. We want everything clean, hygienic and impersonal. We'd rather have a regular, pitiless check from the federal government than be "beholden" to a rich former employer. We'd rather have it written in the contract that we get six days' sick leave annually, than depend on the charity of bosses who have been known (be it remembered) to foot six-month hospital bills.

Furthermore, we train people to be impersonal: Don't be an angel of mercy, be a doctor's assistant. Don't let's let the drug store clerk recommend a headache pill (he can't be trusted), but write to the American Medical Association. Don't advise her as a friend, she'll find it much more beneficial if she pays $10 an hour to consult you. Don't clean Mrs. X's house if it's dirty and she's sick in bed, but refer the case to the domestic service department. Don't preach the love of God, but make laws against discrimination. Put your faith in statistics, reports, committee meetings, money, science, organization, system, technique, methodology—anything, so long as you don't trust people.

Socialization and the planned society are the natural, inevitable result of such de-personalized thinking. Socialism is really just a more thoroughgoing method of eliminating the human element. It will make our lives a hopeless tangle of red tape, which will eventually strangle completely every human effort. No wonder people look back on a vanishing Capitalism with some regret. They think they regret the loss of economic freedom which at least some people had; what they really regret is the loss of the possibility of solving things humanly instead of by a machine. We deserve to get socialism for having given our attention to the perfection of machines and systems instead of men. Affairs will only get worse until we reverse the direction.

In the midst of our plight we have a wonderful example of the wisdom of making *men*, if we would but look. It is the Catholic Church, the only institution in the world which (putting its trust in God) trusts men. A priest is a formed person. A parish curate actually has, and takes, responsibility far in excess of that taken by a first vice-president of a large bank, or the secretary of an enormous insurance company.

The Church also has the key to forming men in secular life. It is Catholic Action, which begins at the beginning the slow, at first painful, finally ever so rewarding, task of making men out of mice.

·4·

The Devil Has It
Both Ways

BEWARE THE MAN who over-simplifies the problem of being
a Christian today. It stands to reason that, since the Western
world is crashing down on our heads, something must be *pro-
foundly* wrong.

Consider how difficult it is to apply the moral law to our
daily life. Who dares say that it is simply a case of our knowing what is right but not doing it? Do we really know what is
right? The *absence* of specific moral direction in social matters
from our pulpits has become an aching void. This is not to
deride the clergy, for a contemporary code of specific social
moral law awaits lay analysis even more than clerical interpretation.

Nor is our plight usually that the Church's law is clear but
entails too much sacrifice—possibly the loss of a job. This is
sometimes the case, but the fact of the matter is that one can
retire from this or that job, this or that hospital or store, but
on the presupposition that there are other jobs and other hospitals where better conditions prevail. This supposition is
largely unwarranted today. It is no longer a question of retreat-
ing, retiring, lifting one's skirts or keeping one's hands clean.

The mess is universal. We are like an army surrounded. Retreat being impossible, we can only fight our way out.

"You're damned if you do, and you're damned if you don't," is really the situation we are most of us in. We are caught on the horns of a dilemma. We are bound, like the gangsters' victims, in such wise that we cannot remain as we are, and struggling only serves to strangle us. The Devil's strategy in our day has been exceedingly clever and is at the height of its success. Whichever way we turn we serve him.

CHOOSE BETWEEN YOUR INTELLECT
AND YOUR WILL
OR
THE DILEMMA OF THE OFFICE WORKER

This is the dilemma of the office worker! he must choose between his intellect and his will, he cannot have both.

Let us say he agrees to forego his intellect. The act of sacrifice consists in taking seriously something which should be treated with levity, if not contempt. In this category we find the grown-up men who seriously deliberate about the exact wording of a subway car-card advertisement for chewing gum. We find the executives who hold luncheons to discuss the plots of comic strips. Then there are all the former idealists who agree, for a consideration, to hold as primary the matter of the profit statement of their companies. There are the radio announcers who degrade themselves by speaking of patent medicines in hushed and hallowed tones. There are the slick writers who produce fiction to formula, and stifle any desire they might formerly have had to spread abroad truth.

Once the sacrifice of the intellect has been made, the will can function within the new framework. A man can get to work on time, be efficient, conscientious, courteous, and indeed practice a sort of asceticism in the pursuit of his false ideal. That is why these people usually appear to have chosen the better part.

They ordinarily make money, are well dressed, are sure of themselves (except in the presence of drinking companions and the psychiatrists they are consulting), and manage to suggest that their personal lives are filled with glamour.

But some men cannot make the sacrifice. They just cannot take seriously enough the childishness, the greed, the stupidities, the red tape, and the imbecility they find in the business world. The sales girl who says to herself, "Why should I sell these ugly, ill-made frocks to this poor dumpy woman?" is of this type, and is (incidentally) finished as a salesgirl. The researcher for TIME (if there be such a one) who would one day observe that it really didn't matter whether or not the names of the first four husbands of an actress now marrying for the fifth time were correctly spelled, would be of this sort. The salesman or advertising genius who reflected that it really didn't matter whether or not people ate cornflakes, the fileclerk who questioned the worthiness of the endless filing of inconsequential letters, the Red Cross worker who doubted the wisdom of sending glamour girls to far corners of the earth for the sake of soldiers' morale; they would all be of this type.

It's a good thing not to give up your intellect, but see what it does to your will if your rebellion is purely negative. If you don't think the game is worth the candle, you will lie in bed in the morning, be inefficient, waste time and watch clocks, and none of these things are virtues (eventually they'll have you at a psychiatrist's too). Worse still, you will be guilty of disloyalty, of breaking a sort of implied contract with your employer. If you beseech Macy's to employ you, have you then a right to engage in subversive activities, to try *not* to sell their goods, or to spread seeds of dissension? Eric Gill speaks of this problem in his autobiography. He was apprenticed to an architect, but he wasted a lot of time talking to co-workers who gave him the real low-down on the state of the architectural profession. He learned more from them than from his master, and eventually gave up architecture on account of what he learned. But he was not proud of his negligence, just the same. He regarded it as a matter of self-preservation.

It would seem to be virtuous to work overtime to help the company out, but what about one's duty to develop one's own talents? One would seem to be bound to apply the conventional rules of salesmanship, but what about the Church's teaching that you have to point out flaws in your product which are not immediately conspicuous, and the general Christian responsibility not to excite the concupiscence of our fellow-citizens?

Belloc contends that the implied contract between employer and employee today is not really a free contract and therefore not binding. This is probably more true in a depression than now. We are practically slaves, but not yet entirely slaves. If we were doing forced labor (and could not be fired, for one thing) we could be subversive to our Christian consciences' content. But since this is not entirely so, we are caught in a moral dilemma. You often hear members of Catholic Action lament that it is *impossible* to do Catholic Action in such and such an office, and hear the answer given them that Catholic Action has *even* been done in concentration camps. But it is easier, morally speaking, to do Catholic Action in concentration camps, because you are there by force, and are not tormented by conflicting loyalties and conflicting moral obligations. In our economy, which is neither slave nor free (but combines the worst features of both systems), the Devil still has it both ways.

IS IT A SIN NOT TO JOIN A LABOR UNION?
OR
ARE LABOR AND MANAGEMENT GENUINE ALTERNATIVES?

It is the Christian who is in the Devil's dilemma, not the socialist. For the socialists the labor unions represent the straight moral path, but is that so for the Christian? The quarrel between management and labor, as such, is one of those quarrels not set in Christian terms, it is a battle over the spoils between adversaries who have no fundamental differences. The essential *agreement* that does in fact exist between labor and management is excellently brought out by Saul Alinsky in *Reveille for Radicals*, a book which has little else to recommend it. They are in essential agreement because they are both essentially materialistic, and it behooves them to make more money by their joint efforts, as preliminary to fighting about who shall get what share of it. Everyone in a shoe factory wants to make more money on shoes, and the question of how the profits shall be divided is only a petty quarrel.

But the way the Devil has arranged things you would think that "to join or not to join a labor union" was a clear-cut moral issue. The fact of the matter is that, universally now, we are materialistic, and it is that which is anti-Christian. To choose the Christian side, the side that stresses the primacy of spiritual values, the side that seeks first the Kingdom of Heaven, the side that looks to God, is to choose the side that doesn't yet exist and the side which, if it did exist, wouldn't exclude the participation of management (and, incidentally, the free exchange of ideas and courtesies between labor and management). The Devil says, "Choose." We can only say, "Yes, I think I will choose, but not between your alternatives. I think I'll choose to be *your* adversary and to start a new movement which will be the antithesis of all you stand for. You divide men by hatred and avarice, I shall unite them in love and godliness. I shall use Catholic Action as my vehicle. It unites men. It starts with the supernatural and works through the temporal order to a supernatural goal. Labor unions will be incidental to it; and not it incidental, and subsidiary to, labor unions."

HOW TO CHOOSE BETWEEN POLITICIANS
OR
IS IT OUR MORAL DUTY TO VOTE?

It is easy to derive the fact that it is one's moral duty to vote. The argument goes like this: You have to be a good citizen, and we live in a democracy where it is the duty of a good citizen to vote. Q.E.D. It is our moral duty to vote.

It sounds so simple. But is it simple? It may become simple soon when one candidate will be overtly communistic, and the other represent a somewhat lesser evil. But at present we have two parties which look very much alike, except perhaps in the distribution of spoils. It may be that the Republican Party is reactionary-capitalistic, and that the Democratic Party tends toward liberalism and socialism. So what? We cannot support the one or the other stand. Both tend ultimately toward loss of freedom and Communism, both are basically godless. So to vote for either, if you see it that clearly, is to lend positive support to a platform contrary to Christian teaching and Papal admonition.

Or, we can vote for the man, and never mind the party. Now there are differences among political candidates, but by and large too many of them are motivated by considerations of expediency, not morality. For a politician to make decisions with an eye on the coming elections is shocking and immoral and contrary to Catholic teaching (which would have him act for the common good). Never mind if everybody does it. It's still gravely reprehensible. How do you choose between two candidates neither one of whom accepts the *primary* duty of his office?

TO LOVE, HONOR AND OBEY
OR
HOW TO BE A GOOD WIFE

It used to be relatively simple to be a wife. You were of the dependent sex. You had pledged yourself to follow, and, save for the unlikely eventuality that your spouse would ask you to rob a bank or stay away from church on Sunday, you could be safe in relaxing and letting your husband make the major decisions and set the tone for the household. Your duty might not always be pleasant; it was at least clear-cut.

But what's the advantage of being a member of the dependent sex if there is no one leading? What's the use of a duty to obey when your husband is as bewildered as you are, if not more so?

Not all men have turned into mice, but something dreadful has happened to the generality of them. Manliness is definitely at a premium these days and one sees instance after instance of weak males whose wives are at least reasonable facsimiles of women of calibre.

It is all right to say that men are sorry specimens because women have been corrupted (through advertising, etc.) and then corrupted them, but is it entirely true? Probably the chief reason for men's degradation is the lack of community life (wherein a man would have found the fulfillment that a woman finds largely in her home), and the ignobility of an industrial-commercial civilization. Men have been robbed of initiative, responsibility and creativity; worse still, they have measured everything in money. Ultimately our degradation can, of course, be traced to the Reformation which has brought about the progressive godlessness of society. An interesting subject for meditation would be the coming into manhood of the medieval and the modern youth: the appalling contrast between the armored knight, pledged to Our Lady, who kept an all-night vigil before the Blessed Sacrament, and the huckster, who spends his last thirty dollars on the hand-painted necktie which will give him entry into his first million.

Women practically cannot help maturing, so close are they to the life forces of humanity. Men can fail to mature their characters even to a ripe old age and death, and this notwithstanding sometimes being married to splendid female specimens.

The moral dilemma, however, falls on the woman. Women are meant to be dependent and to obey men, and it is really a woman's nature, as well as her moral duty, to do so. Women still like manly, commanding men, and always will. However, not having a very penetrating understanding of the present situation, they are trying to escape their dilemma by denying their subsidiary rôle, as witness the feminist movement. You know the cry: "Look what a mess *men* have made of the world, now we women will fix it up." But that's no good (except in parts of Europe perhaps, where there just aren't any men) and wouldn't work. The dilemma is: "women are supposed to obey their husbands, but they cannot obey their husbands because their husbands are too weak to lead them." The solution is not to reverse the order of nature (let men obey their wives) but to make the men strong so their wives can obey them. Part of this duty falls on mothers (to make their sons manly), part of it on wives (to encourage their husbands to independence rather than wealth), but most of it falls on the men.

One of the principles of the modern apostolate is reconversion on a horizontal rather than a vertical plane. The poor will uplift the poor, the school girl will influence the other school girls, the ex-alcoholic will lift his former fellows out of the gutter. This is known as the technique of like-by-like. There is no reason why it should break down when it comes to the sexes. We have too long counted on women to bear the entire burden of the reform of the men. Granted that women do have a profound influence on men, they cannot carry the major burden. Men must encourage each other in recovering their manliness.

SLIPPING BETWEEN THE HORNS OF THE DILEMMA

The only way out of our dilemma is to take resolute action to break down the framework in which the Devil has caught us; to spurn his alternatives in favor of an entirely new departure. Our trouble is that we are trying to fit in where we should be remodelling, trying to follow where we should be leading. What is supremely and immediately necessary today is *Christian initiative* in making a new world. The present world is the Devil's world. Let him have it. Let us strike out anew, break the chains which bind us, impotent, to our files and assembly lines. Let us bring to the workers a new movement impelled by daring ideas of a Christian revolution, and on fire with a love which will draw all men to it. Let us produce statesmen of integrity and of learning and of prayer. Let us produce an entirely new generation of Christian families, with strong, manly husbands and holy, chaste, and obedient wives, to bear saints for the Church.

·5·

Job-Hunting *versus* Vocation

Nothing could be more unnatural by way of discovering one's life work than the current, debasing system of "job-hunting." It would be more dignified, and nearer the true ideal, to be born a slave who grows up to take his place on his master's plantation. At least such a one *has a place*. Back of today's perusal of the want-ad columns, back of today's dreary trek from employment agency to employment agency, back even of the scheming and conniving through one's father's friends for "pull," is the terrifying assumption that one is extraneous to the world's affairs, that there is no place waiting but that an opening has to be hacked in a desperate competitive effort at survival. The Christian idea and the currently accepted method are poles apart. The Christian idea is *vocation*; our commercial reality is *job-hunting*.

We still speak of a vocation to the religious life or the priesthood, but the term used to apply to all occupations. Why was it lost? We lost the sense of vocation, indeed the reality of vocation, in the process of changing from an organic society to a mechanical one, a change which paralleled the development of industrialism (whether or not it was an inevitable consequence

37

of industrialism is beside the point at the moment). In an organic world everyone does what needs doing, what one seems fitted for, and what it is is usually obvious enough. One takes one's place, a place which is already waiting. Péguy somewhere says that he can even remember as a child the last remains of such an organic economic life in France, and that then the workmen went to work singing. In such a society a young man often followed in his father's footsteps, for his father could easily have owned his own farm or his business or his craft. There was a stability in society. One could foresee and prepare for the future. Property and wisdom and skill were passed from generation to generation. Yet it was not a rigid society, provision being made for exceptional vocations, whether religious or scholarly.

Now all that is completely changed. We no longer spontaneously do what needs doing, but we frantically hasten to get in on something which might be making money. For most of us that means finding a place in someone else's scheme for money making. There is no great permanence about the scheme itself, nor do we have security in our jobs from the point of view of being irreplaceable. An enforced security usually involves sacrifice of any interest in the job forever afterwards. If you want to get out of a routine rut you have to swing from limb to limb of the tree of success, always taking chances, always courting disaster. For the most part it is useless to try to follow one's father's footsteps, as he owns nothing and has no particular skill to pass on, but is often just an employee himself. One might as well start at the bottom rung of another ladder, which might even be in another social class. There is no stability anywhere, nor is there even much desire for stability. Little people, as most of us are, with dull jobs, can at least express our dissatisfaction by a restless moving from one stupid job to the next.

THE FACT OF VOCATION

The truth that we need reminding of is that we still all have vocations, that we are still all called by God to do His proper work where He wants us to be. This is what modern youth, almost nurtured on despair, will find it hard to believe. Our failure to believe is the measure of our lack of faith. We must never forget that God is not frustrated, either by bad economic systems, or by atomic bombs, or by seemingly ruined lives. It is always within the power of God to bring good out of evil. Since men of late have disobeyed God, pretty much in a body, the result is that we have made an unprecedented mess of affairs here on earth, and that probably vast numbers of souls have been lost, and are being lost, on account of it. The result is that our *vocations* are ever more insistently vocations connected with the reorientation of things to God. Our vocations are still there. It is just that they are harder to find and to fulfill. When God asks hard things He gives us the grace to do them. We shall need the grace. The key to understanding our times is to realize that mediocrity is impossible: either you are holy or you are lost, either you are with God or you are against Him.

THE UNIQUE NATURE OF TODAY'S VOCATIONS

There is no point in crying over spilt milk or sighing for a more ordered society. You ought not to wish that you were a gently-bred English aristocrat instead of a New York City office girl with a Brooklyn accent. We are called to be saints, not culture vultures; and Brooklynese, previous personal experience as an alcoholic, night-school at Hunter College, and still-unmarried-at-twenty-eight, may prove to be more useful states in the economy of today's salvation than a perfect command of the French language, classical features, or a Ph.D. in Psy-

chology. It certainly would have been unseemly of Joan of Arc
to have refused to command an army on the grounds that a
woman's place is in the kitchen. The important thing is to do
the will of God, to allow ourselves to be called to the vocations
which God wishes, and for which we may find we were re-
motely preparing (according to the mysterious economy of
God's Providence) even in the midst of heartache and dark-
ness. We may not want to live in our own time, but God is
always operating in the present, nor can it truthfully be said
that we are unfortunate in the choice of our generation.
Pius XI thought it a singular privilege to live in such exciting
times. And so it is. It is a time for saints. The thing which is
hard today, which is virtually impossible, is to muddle along.

Certain generalizations can be made about today's vocations,
just from viewing the times. Certain it is that you will not be
swimming with the crowd. You will definitely be going against
the tide—at least until we succeed in changing the direction of
the current. That is why job-hunting is so futile. The sort of
jobs that are open are all jobs within the system, but we have
to change the system, and most of the work will not be done
from within. This is also why the educational system is off the
beam. In general it is preparing us to *fit in*, where it ought to
be preparing us to *make over*.

There will be, and in fact there already is, an increase in
religious vocations to the contemplative life. The Trappist
Monasteries, and the Carmels, are filling up, or are already full.
The penance and prayer therein will form the basis for the
work of those whose vocations are in the world. There will also
be an increase in vocations of suffering in the world. There
certainly is an increase in suffering, which seems to indicate
(to the cancer victims, the starving and the oppressed) a
vocation to suffer willingly that the world may turn again
to God.

There are no real secular vocations today, that is, vocations
to do the work of the world (which could be good in itself, of

course) without regard to religious considerations. This is especially true among the young, and it is what is meant by a general call to the lay apostolate. Today's street cleaner will have to work to convert his fellow street cleaners; today's doctor will have to restore Christian ideals of medicine; today's millionaire will have to start, for example, a movie company to tell of God; today's mother will have to raise saints (and stop undue worry about health, education, and manners); today's writer will have to write the Good News; and vast numbers of us will have to get out of what we are doing or what we are trained to do, in order to initiate or cooperate with some other work we haven't yet dreamt of.

Now the basic reason for this change from secularism is that all the problems that are important problems today are spiritual problems at their roots, and we Catholics have to attack the problems at their roots. That means that not only must we have religious motives and spiritual development, but what we are doing must have as its discernible end the restoration of all things in Christ.

FINDING YOUR VOCATION

As we have said, it is harder than usual to find one's vocation. It is hard because it is hard to know, to find out; and it is hard because it takes sacrifice and faith to accept it. The rules for finding one's vocation can be derived from the word vocation itself. A vocation is, literally, a "calling," and the person who is doing the calling is God. The chief rules are three: 1. Get within earshot. 2. Listen. 3. Believe what you hear.

Rule 1. *Get Within Earshot*

If God is going to speak to us, we have to get near enough to Him to be able to hear. The chief reason that people go around wringing their hands and saying "Oh, I don't know what to do with my life," is that they are spiritually too underdeveloped to find out. Very many people miss their vocations entirely by not developing their spiritual life. What happens is that they try to find out what to do with themselves on a superficial intellectual plane. They decide, in effect, "Wouldn't it be nice for God if I wrote a radio play about His birth, because after all I can write (I've been writing Pepsi-Cola ads for years) and Christmas ought to have a religious note to it." So they write the radio play, and it is done in a very worldly way, using all the usual radio tricks, borrowing a cast from "John's Other Wife," and edifying no one. The unbelievers who happen to tune in are confirmed in their suspicions that Christianity is dull and dead. A few pharisaical church-goers consider that they have pleased God by listening. Meanwhile, a radio-journalist (himself a fallen-away Mormon) hails the playwright as a "prominent Catholic litterateur," which goes to our author's head, and he eventually develops a state of consummate pride.

So the idea is not to think up something nice to do for God, but to approach God with some humility in the hope that He will give you a task. The way to do it is through the Sacraments. Anyone who really wants to learn his vocation ought certainly to start going to daily Mass and Communion if this is at all possible, to go regularly (probably weekly) to confession, to seek out a good spiritual director, to do good spiritual reading and to learn to pray. If no obstacle is put in the way, the Sacraments will act gradually to transform such a person, to make him increasingly docile to the inspirations of the Holy Ghost, to give him more and more insight into contemporary life. From this it can be seen that one cannot find one's vocation overnight. Finding a vocation is not like consulting a job-clinic, where for $10 or so you can take a few tests to learn where you can fit into the system with the least pain and the most profit. No, if you are a person who has not seriously cultivated his interior life to date, it would be well to set aside six months or a year just for the purification process, wherein

the Sacraments have some effect, preferably unmolested by
strong interference from radio and movies.

Rule 2. *Listen*

God shouts. Hearing God's call is not like straining for an
overseas shortwave broadcast. It is perfectly clear and local
once you are within earshot. It is characteristic of the saints
that they are sensitive to the slightest prompting of grace.

Will an inner voice speak? No. God will first of all use
natural means. Chief of these natural means is your *intellect*.
It is absolutely requisite that you start thinking. Start reading
the good Catholic books and pondering them in the light of
your own experience. Start reading up on Catholic Action.
Start asking yourself, or discussing with your friends, the
proper questions about your own life. Ask yourself what you
are doing in your present job, whether or not it has a worthy
end, whether or not it is completely honest. Start meditating on
the Bible. Ask yourself what it means to seek *first* the kingdom
of heaven, to live by *faith*. Thrash all these things out.

Another nudge from God is your *desires*. Now it is the way
of the world to crush all normal desires in the interest of developing dutiful, dull bookkeepers. Try to imagine what you would
do if you were perfectly free, whether it paid or not, and
whether such an occupation already existed or not. If you
have a dull job, just walk out on it for a day sometime to get a
sense of freedom (that is, do this if you are the over-conscien-
tious type. If you are already lax in your duties you had better
work overtime instead, to develop your sense of responsibility).

Usually it is what you once longed for, and never dared
hope for, which was really in line with your vocation. The person who is aching to get married is usually meant to marry. If
you love to take care of the sick, give speeches, teach people,
plant flowers, play instruments or carve statues, that usually
means something. No one has a persistent inner compulsion to
file premium coupons, sort toll-call numbers, watch professional

D

baseball, or talk about silly things in crowded, stuffy, little night-club rooms at wee hours of the morning.

If you can't think of anything you want to do, you are probably suffering from despair. You should cultivate the virtues of faith and hope, and start dreaming again.

If all you want to do is lie on beaches in Florida or sip tall drinks in steamer chairs, you have been thoroughly corrupted by the advertisements and would do well to take a "cure," in the form of giving alms, fasting for Lent and abstaining from mass-circulation magazines. Recreation is not an end in itself.

Besides using your head and your wishes to find your vocation, you must take careful note of *circumstances*. God doesn't say "Yes, Johnny," or "No, Johnny," in so many words. He says them, in effect, in circumstances. If you suffer a severe disappointment, that's usually God saying "No, Johnny." Disappointment in love, loss of your job, failure to get a promotion, especially when these things come through no fault of your own, indicate the will of God, and are therefore blessings in disguise. If we were saints we would praise God for them, seeing that they are all useful toward our final end. All things work together for good for those who love God.

On the other hand, God often gives opportunities, and then He is beckoning us. Seemingly chance meetings with people of like mind, invitations to join Catholic Action groups, and such things God uses to manoeuvre us into our vocations. As a person becomes docile to God's Will, such opportunities present themselves more and more often, and it becomes impossible not to see the guiding hand of God.

RULE 3. *Believe What You Hear*

God does not sit down with you and say, "Now Mary, I want you to found a religious order to take care of some sick people on Easter Island. First I want you to quit your job in the telephone company, then I want you to go to nursing school, then I want you to enter such-and-such a religious order—but you will leave there after six months, it's just to give you train-ing—and then I will arrange for you to have Father X, who is coming over from China, as your spiritual director, and he will tell you about the Easter Island people."

No, God does not tell us where He is leading us. That's the whole point, we have to go from step to step by faith. The supreme thing that God asks of us is faith, that we do not falter or lose confidence while He leads us through the dark-ness. That is why we have to be interiorly developed, to have strong virtues which will keep us from losing confidence. In the days of a Christianly ordered society most men could see clearly where they were going. Now very few of us can see God's way. The pagans think they know where they are going because they are trying to construct the road themselves; but they are in for some surprises.

So in consequence we have to proceed from step to step darkly. If it seems that God badly wants you to quit your job, you had better quit it, even if you haven't got another one. If the next step seems to be washing dishes at $10 a week, wash dishes at $10 a week and be cheerful about it—maybe you are getting some indispensable purification in the matter of pov-erty. If you have to give up your worldly friends, do so without reluctance. Just giving up something that is bad because you are now sure it isn't pleasing to God may be the very act of faith that will start a chain of events leading in the right direc-tion. We live in a world that has faith only in money. We have got to have faith only in God. We have to be instruments, and so our chief virtue must be docility (which is something quite other than the sloth born of despair).

Who has not felt the internal disquiet that comes from pur-suing a course which everyone accepts but which seems phony to you? Who has not sensed the degradation of trying to "sell yourself" to some impressive employment manager? Well, when you set out on your vocation you will have the opposite feel-ing. Everything inside will be in order. You will *feel* you are doing right, and it will make sense to your mind, at least some sense. But outside you may run into a riot. There will be people to tell you that you are betraying your social class. There will be your family to say you are throwing away your chances of success. There will be your father wondering why he sent you to college anyhow.

HOW TO KNOW YOU'VE FOUND YOUR VOCATION

When you get there you will know you have arrived at your goal by the sense of rest and relaxation that will set in. There will be a peace such that it will almost sing out "I belong here," and there will be this peace even if "here" turns out to be on a martyr's gibbet set up in Times Square, or a soapbox set up in front of a howling mob of Communists, or if it turns out to be a cave in a barren waste some place. What's more, you will find that you are not envious of what anyone else is doing, even if it is in itself more interesting or important. All the unengaged girls are envious of the one who captures the local Clark Gable, but let Mary find the man God has chosen for her and whom she sincerely loves, and, be he cross-eyed, she will not covet any other man.

It is plain to be seen that the world's unhappiness is at present greatly intensified by the fact that most people have not found their vocations. As long as you are not in your right place you envy everyone who has any sort of desirable place; everyone wants to be a millionaire, marry a movie actor, get a raise and have an interesting job.

Now the second way to tell you have found your vocation is that the work will come easy to you. It may be building bridges or commanding armies or negotiating peace or editing a newspaper or nursing the insane; no matter how hard these things are in themselves, there will be a naturalness and ease in the way you do them. You will have to work hard, but it will be a pleasure and it won't go against the grain the way things in the past (much easier in themselves) have gone against the grain.

Most of us need kicking upstairs. We make a mess of filing (which, if it must be done, needs a phlegmatic temperament) whereas we would be very good actresses or surgeons. The world's tendency is, since we have so disgracefully failed in filing, to degrade us still further into sorting papers. A lot of neurotics go from bad to worse on this score.

God will, if we trust Him, transport us into some sort of fairyland, better than our wildest dreams. Really that is our big sin against God, that we underestimate Him. We have an inferiority complex about religion when the reality of God is beyond our imagining. We have set our hearts on a new Oldsmobile, whereas eye has not seen, nor ear heard, the things He has prepared for those who love Him. We hope for *so little* for ourselves. The goal that God has set us is to become saints.

·6·

"Emotional" Problems

Have you noticed how many people lately have "emotional" problems? Psychiatrists, psychoanalysts, psychologists, social workers, ministers, and a host of other would-be guides are intent on developing and practicing a "science" for the resolution of emotional problems. Nobody has moral or theological or intellectual or disciplinary problems any more.

One wonders if people know what they are talking about. Is there really any such thing as an *emotional* problem?

WHAT IS AN EMOTION?

Emotions are acts of the sense appetite. They are like feelings, only stronger. They belong strictly to the sense level of man and are the highest activity of his animal nature. They do not belong to the highest part of man, which is purely spiritual. They are inferior to his reason and meant to be governed by reason.

CAN THERE BE EMOTIONAL PROBLEMS?

Emotions are often a problem, but strictly speaking there are no such things as emotional problems in the accepted sense. Emotions just are, and the problems which concern them are

48

always in reference to their government or their proper exercise; that they are running wild, or that the reins are being held too tightly on them. The seat of the trouble, the problem part, is in the intellect or the will. Emotions are like horses, which sometimes run wild. The problem is one of bringing the horses under control, and that is, strictly speaking, the problem of the horse*man*. The reason we talk so much about emotional problems today is because we have forgotten, or denied, that there is a horseman, that men have souls. We only notice the disordered emotions and we are trying to tame them without resorting to horsemen. The results are rather curious.

Besides the relatively simple situation in which you have emotions not curbed at all, or sometimes too tightly curbed, there are other situations, called emotional, to which the emotional aspect is only incidental, or even non-existent. A saner society would instantly have recognized most of our emotional problems as moral or metaphysical problems. Rudolf Allers, the psychologist, says in one of his books that he has never seen a neurotic whose difficulty was not *primarily* metaphysical.

Take the case of the modern pagan young man who doesn't know the purpose of living and so can't keep a job and won't take his place in the world. He suffers from despair and can only be really helped on the religious level. True, despair is an emotion as well as a mental torment, but it is primarily a spiritual difficulty, which gives rise to the emotion of despair. The young man would be tired all the time and feel melancholy, but if you try to cure him with stimulating cold showers or warming glasses of wine or a lot of sleep you will only revive him slightly and then he will relapse. On the other hand, if you can give him hope in God's mercy, his life will take on purpose and the heaviness and fatigue will presently disappear.

Or, consider the case of the married man who falls in love with his secretary. It looks to the modern pagan like an emotional problem, but it is obvious to the most simple Christian that it is not an emotional problem at all but a moral problem which needs to be solved morally, albeit there are emotions aroused which will have to be dealt with.

EMOTIONAL CONTROL

The emotions should be subject to reason, and this, because of original sin, is always difficult. In our day it is often not even tried, and that is one reason why we have so many problems with them. Progressive education has done serious damage in this regard, by trying to make everything pleasant for children and never encouraging them to sharpen their wills on unpleasant tasks.

Emotional control is largely a matter of developing good habits (virtues) in the *will*. That is why proper character education tries always to strengthen the will. Once strengthened it can exercise control over no matter what emotion. This is the principle behind all the Church's mortifications. If a five-year-old child gives up candy for Lent, or an adult fasts, they are building resistance against future temptation not only to gluttony, but also to adultery. We saw during the war the fruits of our self-indulgence. Not many hoped for any display of chastity on the part of the American soldiers (even of most Catholic ones). So the authorities did the only thing you can do if you are not prepared to insist on moral discipline (or if it is too late). They tried to mitigate the social harm, in the matter of disease, which would result from widespread impurity. In so doing they also encouraged impurity, but the basis was already there.

The opposite problem of uncontrolled emotions is that of repressed emotions, a problem which lingers on as a Jansenistic-Victorian heritage. This school thinks there is something bad about emotions as such, so they attempt to repress them entirely, and only succeed in bottling up the physical manifestation of emotions, unhealthily. Emotions are partly physical and partly spiritual, and you cannot choose the spiritual part without allowing for the physical manifestation. If you are angry in your mind, let the blood rush to your head. If you don't, it will rush to your stomach and you will get ulcers. The only cure for unwarranted anger is to turn your mind to other considerations. So it is with sex. Purity consists, as the Church has always maintained, in having a pure mind as well as pure actions. If you desire impurity in your mind but refrain from carrying out your desires, you not only sin, but you are always liable to become a neurotic. Modern psychology would find you inhibited and frustrated and a lot of other things. Today it is even difficult for married people to be pure, because our society has allowed temptations to be presented from every billboard and in the dress of all the clerks in offices. Freudian psychoanalysts wax wealthy caring for people who do not lead sensuous lives, but who wish they did (perhaps subconsciously) because the prevailing opinion of our pagan society is that the absence of sense pleasure is a deprivation because sensuality is the highest good. You cannot entirely blame the Freudians if they have deified sex, since it is partly because we have distorted the ideal of purity.

The answer to the Freudians is to regain the proper ideals. Emotions should be seen as good things if properly ordered. Among the young adults today, Catholic and non-Catholic, you find that there is scarcely one of them who was instructed in the facts of life by his parents. This situation is now being remedied by preparation for marriage courses and the instruction of adults in the instruction of their children, so there will not be another lost generation. Our parents must themselves have been very much the victims of Jansenism and puritanism to have been so conspicuously negligent. The results are all too apparent and appalling. When you learn of things surreptitiously (and often erroneously) you develop a false sense of shame, followed by an "emotional" problem or by a reaction in licentiousness.

SENTIMENTALITY

Sentimentality is one of the worst effects of our preoccupation with feelings in disregard of the higher faculties. Sentimentality is this: an effort to decide on the level of feeling what we should be deciding with the intellect. It is a good thing to have feelings, but it isn't a good thing to let them rule your reason.

One wonders if there has ever been a more sentimental age than ours. If you read through a magazine like the *Reader's Digest* you feel as though you had been through an emotional orgy. You don't come out with intellectual light but with emotional fatigue. It's full of stories of poor stray dogs and noble urchins and brave dipsomaniacs. Many of our highest-paid American writers have fallen completely into the groove of distorting facts, or imagining circumstances, that will pull heart strings. They unconsciously strive to give us emotional satisfaction instead of clear facts or principles.

Even *Time* magazine goes in for this. They reported a year or so ago the story of a brave little G.I. who lost his life striving to save someone who fell off a bridge over Niagara Falls, and in the *Time* tale the G.I. (who was traveling alone) had been watching the falls and meditating pretty thoughts about his imminent homecoming. *Time* didn't know, of course, what he had been thinking about, but the sentimental American public must have a hero made to order in this fashion. They couldn't have reconciled his meditating on, say, the fact that the square on the hypotenuse of a triangle is equal to the sum of the squares of the other two sides. This example, incidentally, is from St. Thomas, a man who could reconcile such a thing. It is St. Thomas who says, against the probability that men in general make acts of love of God at the moment of death, that they might be reflecting on a geometrical law.

Sentimentality, since it makes the senses the high court,

judges all things on the material level. So we pity the tenement dweller, and envy the Stork Club habitué, but if we lived by Faith, we would weep in the reverse order. It is because of this sentimentality, indeed, that we have come to believe that poverty (not destitution, just poverty) is about the greatest of human ills, and that happiness lies somewhere in the direction of a Bendix.

Social workers now think it is very important to "love" their clients. So it is, but love formerly meant charity and now it means some vague sort of emotion. Love of the poor is in reality a harsh and terrible thing (it has been said by those who know that they are often an ungrateful and trying lot), to be achieved only by great charity, that is to say, holiness. Instead we have this mock charity which manifests its "love" chiefly by abstaining, often in a culpable manner, from moral judgments and advice.

Sentimentality has nowhere betrayed us as it has in medicine. One's pity (an emotion) immediately goes out to those in pain, and this is good as long as it doesn't interfere with a person's higher good or higher duty. The three worst contemporary abuses of modern medicine can be traced directly to sentimentality—to a misguided pity. They are birth control, euthanasia, and the habit of deceiving the dying about the imminence of their death.

REALISM

Why is it that the new cult of "realism" is so brutal? Is real life just one big sewer? No. The realists, so called, are reacting without enlightenment against the sugary unreality of sentimentality. There is a basic hypocrisy about sentimentality (always coloring facts to get an emotional response), which eventually nauseates, and the realists represent the vomit of a society thus sickened.

Realism is also emotional, but it evokes the strong and

brutal emotions instead of the gentle ones. Realism fails too to rise above the level of sense to reason which alone can give reality to our picture of the world.

If you see realism for what it is, the reaction of a sickened public to saccharinity, you will understand why it is that the masses of men can turn quickly from being gentle and docile to mass brutality. You can see too why romances of the lovey-dovey sort so quickly turn after marriage into mutual revulsion and castigation.

The Church offers an interesting example of the attraction-revulsion, and finally the resolution of an emotional quandary in regard to devotions. Owing to a long-time progressive separation of devotion from theology, Catholic devotions, including church music, fell into a sentimental morass. The reaction was a turning away from the Church, especially among men. You still rarely see men at services other than compulsory Mass, and in some national groups, not even at that. The recovery began with the restoration of the liturgy, and particularly of the Chant, which has the virtue of integrating the emotions with the worship of God, not as exploiting them, but as subordinating them, as a vehicle for raising the mind and heart to God.

HOW DO YOU SOLVE EMOTIONAL PROBLEMS?

Proof that the so-called emotional problems are not really emotional is that you cannot solve them on the emotional level. See what has happened to those trying to solve them in disregard of the higher faculties.

You will never get a clear-cut answer from a Freudian psychoanalyst about how he knows when he has cured anyone. Let us return to the analogy of the wild horse, with the problem of how to quiet him without resorting to a horseman. You can just let him loose to do what he pleases, and that will at least end the struggle. He will be happy as long as you don't try to bridle him, but he will also be useless to you. So it is with human beings, only worse. There are those whose solution to emotional problems seems to be just to follow the emotions around, letting them do what they please. In this way they are useless in regard to higher purposes than emotional satisfaction, and in time fail even to give that. Furthermore, men are not animals and cannot stand up indefinitely under emotional indulgence. If you let a man wallow in his despair, he will finally kill himself or get schizophrenia, and if you let a person whose difficulty seems to be sex be as promiscuous as he pleases, he will end up in despair or insanity, not to mention a number of difficulties he will encounter en route.

Another method of solving emotional problems is bribery. This is an effort to circumvent the will. Instead of trying to please the emotions you try to please the will. You make a person *want* to do this or that, usually by bribing him with things pleasing to the senses. From this wild, and really incoherent, theory, you get things like the contemporary fingers pointed at nasty parents who don't make it *pleasant* for Junior to stay at home. It is true that the modern home is not conducive to domesticity but it is not on grounds of pleasure that it can be condemned, but on grounds of loss of function. Coca-Cola in the refrigerator and a juke-box in the living room won't help. And in any case the problem of Junior and his lack of discipline remains.

Or, you can destroy the conscience, or at least try to. This is the main attack on conflicts regarding morality. Freud tried something of the sort with talking. Lately they are trying to do it with surgery. This is what the lobotomy operation, featured by *Life* magazine, claims to do. It is an interesting piece of reasoning that its advocates go through. Since Mr. X has a conflict between what he ought to do and what his emotions want him to do, let's destroy the sense of ought. But the sense of ought, the conscience, is the intellect itself, in relation to its practical moral judgments. You can't destroy the conscience without impairing the mental faculties, and it sometimes seems (although full data is not available) that this is exactly what they are doing.

THE DECLINE OF MAN

All these errors about emotional problems could not have arisen in a vacuum. They represent not so much the aberrations of a few men as a major sign of the disintegration of human beings. Here we are: men trying not to be rational animals but to operate on the level of emotional animals— men who have stepped down from their level of human beings.

This is a terrible sign of the times. It is not so terrible to have bad men in an age which recognizes and develops intellects and wills. It is an awful thing to have men so ignorant, so undisciplined and weakened, that they are almost incapable of sinning, because they are almost not men at all.

·7·

Last Things First

WE'LL *never get to the roots of the ills of society today if we consider acts and things in themselves alone and not also in their ordering. Sometimes it makes all the difference in the world merely what is put first and what last.*

THE SIN OF CURIOSITY

Curiosity is one of those sins which are today hailed as virtues. Everyone knows it's wrong to peek through keyholes, but most people think it's laudable to try to learn and learn in the manner exalted by liberal colleges. It will come to many as a surprise to learn that intellectual curiosity is a sin. The reason is that they think intellectual curiosity is a love of truth, whereas in reality it is a disordered lust for knowledge. The sin of curiosity concerns the ordering of knowledge. It means *seeking to know secondary things before you know primary things*. It is wanting to know all about the burial customs of the early Egyptians before you know the meaning of death. It is gathering statistics on tenement conditions before you know the uses of poverty. It is studying "guidance" before you know the purpose of life. It is doing historical research before you know the beginning and end of all things. It is reading Freud before you know whether or not man has a soul. It is trying to find out what the world is made of without knowing or caring who made it.

Why should it be a sin to study second, third, eighth or tenth things before you know first things? I don't know if the Church has said exactly why it is a sin (and not, for instance, just a stupidity), but one can speculate that it is because curiosity is against nature, a perversion. It is against the nature of the intellectual faculty. We are made in such a way that we have to know the most universal and general things first, afterwards less universal things, and individual things only indirectly and through the senses. If you did not know the species "dog" first (the mind has the power to abstract this concept), then you could only see, feel and smell this particular mongrel, without understanding anything about him. Likewise, you have to know that death is the separation of the soul and body before you can understand why the body disintegrates and why the personality of your friend has vanished; otherwise you will be just mystified and terrified by lifelessness and corruption.

THE FOLLY OF OUR INTELLECTUALS

Now the sin of curiosity produces a sort of folly among learned men. A simple, illiterate, Christian peasant (if there are any left) could easily confound most of our college presidents, because the peasant would know first things anyhow, according to the capacity of his mind, so that he would have the outline of life correctly drawn and his judgment, though crude, would be essentially correct. The college president, on the other hand, would have a head stuffed full of uncorrelated facts, or facts mechanically sorted. He would know what Plato taught, what Aristotle taught, what Spinoza taught, what Hegel taught and what Bertrand Russell teaches; without knowing what of it is true and what is erroneous. It is because of this blindness, because of this absence of wisdom in the midst of learning, that a dull student with a good memory, whose only desire is to get a degree and so a job, does well in college. The seeker of truth usually does better on his own.

SCIENCE AND THE SENSES

The reason people turn to the study of the sciences is that there lies, if not wisdom, at least knowledge that is concrete, true as far as evident, and often useful. That is because science is concerned for the most part with sense data, with individual observable and measurable things, and hardly touches the speculative intellect. A man with a neat, dictionary-type mind, can spend his life catching butterflies and arranging them all in neat trays according to family likenesses, and feel that he has contributed something worthwhile to mankind. And, indeed, he has made a contribution of a very minor sort. Meanwhile he can be an irritable old grouch, narrow and selfish, quite lacking in wisdom and puerile in his opinions on primary things. Or, he may try to rise through his little knowledge of secondary things to first things and decide, for instance, that the world was originally a cocoon from which we all emerged. This is the sort of error to which scientists are liable. First things are the province of theologians and philosophers, to which scientists ought to defer (though no one can blame them for not deferring to liberal philosophers and Protestant theologians, with whom they are generally most familiar. The deference is understandably usually the other way around). First things do not respond to the scientific method, and scientists look very foolish when they try to make them do so. Einstein only looks silly when he is pontificating on the non-existence of the Deity. The evolutionary hypothesis is an error of just this sort. When men found out the exquisite order of creation they jumped, illogically, to the conclusion that higher forms of life had developed from lower, whereas religious men would have accepted this diversity and order as reflecting multitudinously the unique perfection of God.

E

THE SCIENTIFIC METHOD

It is interesting to compare the scientific method, which is based on inductive reasoning, with deduction, which is more consonant with our rational nature. Deductive reasoning is syllogistic, proceeding from the universal principle to the particular application, or from the more universal to the less universal. The so-called "scientific method" tries to rise from particulars to universal truths, which is often harder, nor do good scientists always do this, even though they think they do. What happens is that a gifted scientist has a "hunch," which he uses as an hypothesis, a universal proposition, and then tests it out. Experimentation is a way of verifying the first premise, but the hunch comes first.

Take the case of cancer, for instance. An awful lot of money is being expended in cancer research, but whether it is being intelligently used or not is another question. The scientific method would be to get exhaustive data about everything concerning the patients, and then hope to see some universal precondition which existed. This would give happy results only more or less by accident. The deductive approach would be for a wise and profound doctor to speculate more or less at random on the basis of his experience, with the hope of making a sort of intuitive synthesis to use as an hypothesis. For this you need good doctors more than good equipment. A meditation might go something like this: "Let's see. Cancer only gets started in weak tissue; now, what would cause weak tissue? . . . It's a deficiency of some sort and one much more frequent today than formerly. Let's see. What conditions peculiar to today could conceivably cause it? . . . Well, there's smoking, there's adulterated food, there's nervous tension, there are chemical fertilizers . . . Let's try some of these hypotheses."

Given such a basis, controlled experiments might prove very fruitful, and could be done with the minimum of data gathering and of discomfort to patients, not to mention expense.

THE PSEUDO-SCIENCES

Out of an over-emphasis on science, and a neglect of theology and philosophy, is arising an extremely dangerous condition in the intellectual field. There just has to be some ordering of knowledge or men will be swimming in a chaos. At present there are two movements. One is to revive philosophy and theology. The other is to invent a philosophy on the basis of science. Yale University has recently revised its entire curriculum to emphasize science more, and seemingly to invent a scientific sort of philosophy to fit the facts. This very unfortunate tendency has been going on for some time. One evidence has been the institution of the pseudo-sciences, notably psychology and sociology.

There is such a thing as a valid psychology, which is really a sub-division of philosophy (that's why psychology was at first under the philosophy departments in colleges), and which starts with philosophy's knowledge of the nature of the soul. What is usually taught in secular colleges, however, is something quite different; a combination of what is measurable in men's actions, and the gratuitously assumed general principles of practicing psychiatrists and psychologists, the most notable being those of the atheist-materialist, Freud. But psychology purports to be the study of the soul (they call it the psyche), which is essentially unmeasurable, because it is a spiritual substance without bulk or extension. So what happens?

In the field of experimental psychology much that is discovered is something everybody knew all along (such as that Mary Jane has manual dexterity, and that Johnny has a good memory), or that doesn't very much matter. Psychological tests of the intelligence are moderately useful for making rough judgments of strangers. They are relatively accurate as long as they are measuring the physical factors which influence intelligence or ability. For instance, imaginative and cogitative powers depend on the physical structure of the brain, and the excellence (also the kind) of one's intellect is partly dependent on them. With memory the case is a little different. The intellectual faculty (which is purely spiritual, remember) stores ideas and principles which it can call to mind for future use, and this accumulated wisdom cannot be estimated by psychological tests, although it would be brought out by a philosophical or theological examination of the right sort. But there is also a sensory power of memory, seated in the brain. This is what is measured by "nonsense syllables," and it only indirectly affects the excellence of the intelligence.

The other branch of psychology concerns the soul proper. Here the emphasis is on mental health. Here is where you need first of all a knowledge of what the soul is, and that must come from philosophy and theology. In practice it is taken from Freud et al. who have really invented philosophies of sorts, sensual and materialistic. They were wrong, and therefore the pseudo-sciences erected on their premises are wrong, more wrong on the whole than experimental psychology. We had a good example of this in wartime, in the psychiatric tests given to men called to the service. They consisted of lurid explorations of the sexual nature of the men, with little or no attention given to exploring their religious orientation. It was a system which made a devout soldier look like a psychopath, and purity seem like a neurosis. Psychiatry will never be on the right track until it is rooted in the real nature of man. Until then its cures will all be of an accidental nature.

SOCIOLOGY

Sociology represents another attempt to acquire through measuring and counting the wisdom proper to theology and philosophy. Sociology is really not a science, but should be a sub-division of moral theology; that part concerned with the moral principles affecting men in society. Take one question which preoccupies sociologists, that of population. One ought properly to begin considering this subject with certain principles in mind, such as that contraception is unnatural, marriage is indissoluble, and that God Who asked us to propagate must have known what He was about. If then you studied population trends and factors affecting the population, you would come out with recommendations for family housing, decentralization of urban populations and such. But if you start the other way around, to examine conditions with what you think to be an open mind, but what is really a mind open to the unconscious suggestion of all your own opinions, prejudices and emotions, you will (if you are the modern pagan materialist) come up with solutions in the nature of birth control. Pagan sociology now has, as a matter of fact, a complete set of the wrong answers: contraception, abortion, euthanasia, divorce, beehive housing and social security.

FIRST THINGS AND NEUROSES

You have to know the first things before you can understand second things, otherwise you live in mental confusion, or on the sense level. Now this mental confusion often takes the form of neurosis. That's why you find so many maladjusted college students reading Nietzsche. They are looking for an answer, in the wrong place to be sure, but still looking. The most merciful thing that can be done to a neurotic is to give him truth and light. If he's not already too mixed up, you will see the joy that comes from receiving an intelligible explanation, providing it *is* intelligible and stated in terms that mean something in his own life.

The primary cause of neurosis is intellectual confusion rather than, as some maintain, emotional disturbance, although emotional elements are mixed up with it or follow from it. Freudian "cures" result chiefly from the fact that Freud offers a plausible, though erroneous, explanation of neurotic conduct.

It is in the light of ignorance of first things that we ought to have great sympathy for pagans who become neurotic. They often are the best people, the ones who have not succumbed to the sin of curiosity, and who decline to invent a philosophy of sense pleasure. They hold out for the first principles and, failing to receive them, they go to pieces.

THE PUNISHMENT OF INTELLECTUAL CURIOSITY

The punishment of the sin of curiosity is very severe. It is called "spiritual blindness," and it consists in this, that God takes away light from our understanding. It then becomes not so much a matter of men's not wanting to find the truth as it is of their not being able.

Spiritual blindness is the disease which affects very many of the liberal educators and the liberally educated. These people cannot even see their own logical errors. They are those with whom it is almost useless to argue, and for whom it is imperative to pray.

If Catholics are persecuted here (as, please God, they will not be) these spiritually blind guides will probably be the ones to mete out judgment. It is consoling to think (for it is obvious that they will foster our martyrdom) that they were Christ's judges too.

· 8 ·

Collector's Item

W<small>E HAVE MADE</small> *a fetish out of the unusual. Let a man be born with six toes and we are full of wonder, who have not yet learned to appreciate five toes. When people cease to appreciate the usual, they have an unhealthy curiosity about the unusual.*

EXOTIC NATURALISM

Let us call this perversion "exotic naturalism," and let us suppose, because it may be true, that the Devil has fostered this attitude in us in order to prevent nature from doing what nature strongly tends to do: raising our hearts and minds to the creator of nature. Louis of Granada, a Spanish Dominican of several hundred years ago, wrote a book which would sound naive to the ordinary zoology student but which shows the simple wonder which God's creation arouses in the guileless. How marvelous of God to have provided this animal with so warm a coat to withstand the hard winter and those birds with such sure instincts for building nests!

To return to the Devil. He has, if it is he, persuaded us that orchids are less lovely in Havana, where they are common, than in Manitoba, where they are rare; that strawberries are more remarkable in January than in June when they are in season, and that a Bedlington dog is much to be preferred to a fox terrier because there are fewer Bedlingtons. It is with pride that a man says: "I am the only person who has ever captured a copperhead snake in this section of Connecticut." It is with humility that a man views the copperhead simply, and wonders at the God who made it, or even why He made it. It is a clever or lucky one who finds a *four*-leaf clover, but we tend to forget that God most consistently reveals a tiny bit of Himself in clovers with leaves of the usual number.

ANTIQUES

Another example of prizing what is rare is in the matter of antiques. Here it is a different lesson we fail to grasp.

Does it not seem odd that furniture made several hundred years ago should be valued far above that made yesterday? When you think about it, it even seems odd that furniture made several hundred years ago should have out-lasted furniture made yesterday. The glaring fact back of the modern craze for antiques is seldom mentioned. It is that we can't make as good furniture today as our ancestors made. Ours isn't as beautiful, as durable, or as skillfully fashioned. As craftsmen and wood-workers and artists we moderns are on the down grade. It looks as though we've been on the down grade for a long time. As far back as living memory goes furniture has grown old, or become second-hand—never antique.

The same thing that occurs in regard to furniture also takes place in regard to architecture. Some ten years or so ago a whole row of houses on Washington Square in New York was rebuilt, with elaborate care taken to preserve the original façade. For these were among the most beautiful in New York. They were built in the early 19th century. We can't make anything comparable now. This goes also for the colonial architecture which the late Henry Ford and others so carefully restored. P.S. 68 is already an eyesore, while the little red school house has become a museum.

In England this process of preservation of old churches, abbeys and houses has been a matter of public concern for many years. Most of the English architectural gems date back to pre-Reformation times. In a recently published account of the life of Blessed Margaret Clitheroe (a Reformation martyr), Margaret Munro mentions that Blessed Margaret's house is still to be seen in York and is one of the most beautiful houses in England. Blessed Margaret was a butcher's wife, she taking her turn keeping the shop. Even a butcher in those days lived in a more beautiful house than it is possible to build today. From sturdy, roomy architectural loveliness to quonset hut— civilization marches on!

MUSEUMS

Can it be a coincidence that museums look like tombs? Or are they really tombs of dead culture? There is a reason for an occasional museum to preserve such historical paraphernalia as Indian flints, or astronomical curiosities like meteors. But our museums bear too much testimony to the passing of a living culture. This is nowhere more evident than in their collections of religious art. By what curious process have pictures of Our Lady and lovely crucifixes found their way into the Metropolitan Galleries? It seems sacrilegious—indeed it is, in a way —to stand coldly, like a sightseer, before Christ on the Cross, presumably noting the skill with which the wood carver has fashioned the agony on Our Lord's face. And that beautiful painting over there—oughtn't there to be a prie-dieu in front of it?

You have only to leave the museum and hasten to the nearest church to be repelled by the currently used religious art.

Why is there this divorce between religion and artistic creativity today? Where are the religious artists? Happily there are a few, and the number is increasing. But most of the artistic gifts of the nation are still employed on behalf of soap advertisements. In an age dominated by commerce the best talent will be building skyscrapers and photographing baked beans. In an age preoccupied with God they would have been building cathedrals and painting madonnas. There is a direct correlation between the advertising pages of the *Ladies' Home Journal* and the cheap machine-made stations of the cross in the parish church.

How did religious art find its way into the museums anyhow? In Russia the Communists confiscated the beautiful vessels and vestments of the Orthodox Church (they were declared state property and the priest whose chalice was stolen had to pay damages to the atheist state, but many of the best were just stolen). Lovely old icons are on display in peoples' museums, with appropriate derogatory remarks about their former usage. Beautiful Russian vestments and liturgical books can even occasionally be seen in Fifth Avenue shop windows, courtesy of the Soviet Embassy. There is no stigma attached to stealing religious goods. It would be interesting to know how much of the religious art in our museums was stolen by the irreligious governments of France, Spain, Mexico and the rest. I have heard of a man living in an old English house, formerly one of the buildings connected with a monastery, who suspected he knew where the monks had hidden the sacred vessels when they were forced to flee under Henry VIII. Permission from the government was necessary in order to make the search. But he, being a Catholic, was reluctant to look, for by law the vessels would become the property of the English crown, and very likely also of the English Church. When you consider all the persecutions the Church has endured it is not hard to conjecture how art found its way from Church to museum.

THE LUNATIC FRINGE

I once met a man whose life was dedicated to the collection of pre-canceled one-cent stamps. He spent a good part of his income buying up huge lots of used stamps in the hope of discovering one pre-canceled by a town not already in his collection. His family's bathing habits were restricted by his frequent use of the bathtub for soaking the stamps off the envelopes. At intervals he met with other collectors of pre-canceled stamps, gathered in convention from all over the United States.

This poor man represented the collector's mania as purely maniacal. Pre-canceled one-cent stamps are not beautiful, are not useful, are not educational, contain in themselves no excuse for accumulation. My friend was one with the collectors of bottle tops and match covers. He should be a salutary warning to all philatelists and those who bring home pretty stones and shells from the beach. These harmless, faintly educational collections are all right as hobbies, but beware of their becoming obsessions in an age that has lost its balance. Already stamp-collecting has lost its amateur charm. Government post office departments make stamps out of deference to collectors, and in the interests of money making. You don't have to wait until you or your neighbor gets a letter from Pago-Pago, the post office will arrange it for you. No polar expedition is complete without its sop to the philatelists. Stamp collecting is about as simple and guileless as a serpent these days.

LOOKING OVER OUR OWN SHOULDERS

How has it come about that the simple joy of collecting things has become warped and diseased? Well, one reason is that already mentioned; there is an element of the fanatic in it because creativity is so nearly dead. This vase, chair, hand-bound book, or lovely icon is *irreplaceable*. Not just nice or useful or beautiful in itself, but the product of dead genius.

The other reason is that in a godless age all things lose proportion and balance. We have lost our perspective and a sort of self-worship, collective pride, threatens. Maybe this is why we don't admit that the antiques put us to shame. We continue to collect them while bragging about the superiority of our own age. Since our own furniture, pots and pans, and houses will certainly not even endure long enough to become antiques, we have turned to other items from which to seek the enduring glory of our age.

St. John of the Cross says that the proud man is always watching himself instead of watching God. He's always looking over his own shoulder. That's a good description of our society. Notice our contemporary self-conscious manipulation of history. It used to be that looking back in history we could see that seemingly obscure events had immense future significance. Nowadays we write everything in scarlet letters in future history books before the event ever happens. The San Francisco conference of several years ago (already lost in oblivion) was heralded as certain to go down in history with significance. Mr. So-and-So's diplomatic trip to Moscow (by the way, who *did* go to Moscow?), or John Smith's name in the paper, what are they anyhow? When we who are now living are all dead, someone is going to find a lot of fountain pens around, each one having written a third of a word on a peace treaty that didn't bring peace, or a bill which unfortunately passed and then couldn't be enforced. These, together with the curious paraphernalia of a few "time capsules," will constitute our own premeditated "relics." They will look pretty silly beside the genuine relics of the saints among us whom nobody knows and who have never been on an audience-participation program on the radio.

It is salutary to remember what made Pontius Pilate go down in history.

·9·

Birth Control

İT DOES look, to the superficial view, as though Catholicism will be able to do in America, and in the twentieth century, what has hitherto been impossible to it, and what Christ said was impossible. It looks superficially as though we Catholics could ride with the tide of Americanism, flourish and prosper, increase and multiply, and even gradually win the respect and conversion of our fellow citizens—all this without martyrdom, singularity, misunderstanding or ostracism. Indeed we seem already to have arrived at such a state. You will find Catholics prominent in almost every field now, working beside non-Catholics without discrimination, in factory, office and examination room, on wards and in laboratories. You will also find that these Catholics who have in such large numbers "arrived" at respectability and comfort and country club membership, resent the "radical" elements within the Church which disturb the neat compromise they have made. Are the "radicals" really wrong? Are things going as nicely as they seem to be going?

The fly in the ointment of complacent Catholicity is a secret sin. It is the practice of contraception. Underneath the polite veneer, behind the lip service to religion, beyond the hundreds of little compromises with principles on the grounds that "everyone is doing it" and "I am no theologian" (nor have I any intention of learning enough theology to make myself uncomfortable); back of this whole façade, and in the privacy of marital relationships, there comes a black-and-white choice on a grave moral matter.

How many Catholic couples practice contraception? There are no figures, of course, but among young couples in urban districts would it be an exaggeration to place the figure at over fifty per cent? There is quite a bit of evidence, of an informal sort. The scarcity of babies is the most telling evidence. No judgment can be made in individual cases, but a sort of general judgment *must* be made. When a mammoth housing project has a high percentage of Catholic families, and when these families characteristically cease to increase beyond the point where the walls of their three rooms cannot well encompass an addition to the family, what is the natural conclusion to be drawn? In such a housing project, where such a situation prevailed, the authorities declined to allow moving from three- to five-room apartments within the project, preferring to fill the five-room vacancies from without. Was a petition against this prohibition made by Catholic parents of growing families in the name of morality? There was not! Meanwhile, the local parishes were bursting with pride at their well-heeled, generous and enthusiastic parishioners. But privately among the married women there was a new moral code developing. Those who, practicing contraception, also refrained from receiving the Sacraments, held themselves as morally superior to those who, in the same state of mortal sin, committed the sacrilege of making bad Confessions and receiving Communion.

Or take another case. In Connecticut, where the birth control issue is hotly contested politically, a young pagan doctor told me that non-Catholic engaged couples appreciate receiving information on contraception, but Catholic ones insist upon it. The Planned Parenthood Association is very strong in this same state. Its clinics are not without a sizable Catholic clientele.

But the best evidence is from priests giving parish missions.

Contraception is the major obstacle to the spiritual health of one parish after another up and down the country. The priests not only have to fight the practice of birth control but also the growing tendency of Catholics to excuse themselves from culpability because of the prevalence of this moral disorder.

What is the nature of this hidden corruption which is eating away at our Catholic life, secretly corrupting the Mystical Body?

BIRTH CONTROL IS UNNATURAL

The Church is against artificial contraception because it is a perversion of nature, because it is a radical abuse of a natural faculty. God made sex for purposes of procreation, and added pleasure to its exercise as a sort of incentive and reward for perpetuating the race. When you see it this way you are forced to be grateful to God Who has fashioned nature so as to make duties enjoyable, and Who has attached to this supreme duty in the natural order (supreme, that is, for mankind, but not for every individual) the most intense pleasure in the physical order. How diseased men's minds have become in that they now consider the pleasure of sex as some sort of right of theirs to which no duties are attached. They even think that the natural fruit of marriage, that for which marriage was instituted, destroys the perfection of their married love.

It is customary for theologians to compare the practice of artificial contraception with a Roman custom known as the "vomitorium," wherein gluttonous men feasted until they could eat no more; then they made themselves sick so as to empty their stomachs and start over again. Like the modern who practices birth control, they wanted only the pleasure of their acts. But God made eating delightful primarily to ensure our nourishment, and it is therefore sinful to frustrate the normal consequence of the act. The parallel with contraception is exact.

Since it is unnatural, therefore artificial contraception is in itself sinful, and those who hope that the Church will relax her prohibitions hope in vain. It is not within the power of the Church to change the natural law.

DECADENCE AND DESPAIR

Propagandists for the Planned Parenthood Association claim that artificial contraception is not a new thing but that it was practiced by all the great civilizations. So it was—just before they went under. It is one of those practices which characterize dying societies. There are a whole set of signs of decadence which are like the signs which presage the death of a man. A corrupting society will show a general moral breakdown. A fundamental despair will pervade, and manifest itself, among other ways, in suicides. It came to be considered in ancient Rome that a man had no right to interfere with his neighbor's killing himself, and if you saw him cut his own throat in the street, you let him be. Another sign of despair is frantic pleasure-seeking, not least of all in lust. It is out of overindulgence of natural functions, out of the jaded appetites which it produces, that unnatural vices are born. Two of these, and they are usually found together, not in the same persons but in the same city populations, are homosexuality and contraception (along with abortion). These are rampant in our society.

It may seem to some as though the Church were clinging to a meaningless prohibition which is holding back the wheels of human progress and happiness. When you see contraception in its context, as one of a number of serious moral disorders characterizing decadent societies, you see the glory of the Church's stand. She is now quite alone in defense of the moral law in respect to contraception. Anyone who reads the popular press can see how close society is to lauding those other disorders—euthanasia, suicide, homosexuality, and abortion. How wonderful it is to know that the Catholic Church will stand firm against all these sinful practices, even if the whole rest of the world sinks into them. Her stand on the matter of birth control is our guarantee that she will always remain firm.

THE PERSONAL DILEMMA

Seeing how right the Church is in the matter of contraception does not in itself resolve the dilemma of the young married couple. It only puts the problem in relief, for the truth of the matter is that the ordinary couple can't go along with our society (even if their ambitions are moderate) and also have all the children God may send them. Everything in our society conspires against the normal family. There is first of all the matter of housing. Apart from the sometimes immoderate cost, and the present dire shortage, it is true (it has been true for years) that the modern house or apartment is made to planned parenthood specifications. Apartments have given way to housing projects, and individually built houses have deferred to large-scale community planning. You are invited to conform— or else. Conformity means three rooms, or a match-box cottage just the right size for a honeymoon.

Or take the wage system. When men were independent owners of farms or small stores, children rapidly became an economic asset. Now they are a liability until their full maturity. Meanwhile most fathers are wage slaves, and nowhere in our country (so far as I know) is there a wage differential in respect of families. All men inspecting gears as they pass down the automobile assembly line are paid alike, say fifty-five dollars a week. Obviously Joe Jones, who is single, does rather better financially than Bill Smith next to him, whose wife is expecting her seventh child.

The matter of social life is also rough on prolific couples. Gone are the days when parents or maiden aunts lived in the same spacious house, or nearby, and helped mind the children.

F

Gone too is neighborliness. And also gone are family parties. All that remains is a persistent baby-sitter problem.

Babies are more expensive too. Just having a baby costs around one hundred dollars minimum now in large cities for the doctor. Hospitalization (and everybody goes to the hospital) is at least as much again. About a generation ago the whole thing could be done for thirty-five dollars. All sorts of factors have been influential in raising the cost of having babies to this unprecedented height. It will be a complex situation to unravel.

Let us consider just one more of the reasons why children and modern living are antagonistic. It is the matter of bourgeois living standards. It amounts to this: in a thousand ways there is pressure put upon us to live on a scale which automatically precludes babies, at least in any quantity.

Before the war there was a study made which showed this antithesis very clearly. Bank clerks in England were taken as the subjects because their wages were fixed, their years of apprenticeship established, and they were good exemplars of white collar work. Bank clerks had to present a certain appearance which presumably reflected the dignity and stability of banking but was not at all in keeping with the salaries of the clerks. The investigation clearly showed that the clerks were actually forced both to late marriage and to the practice of contraception by the circumstances and salaries of their work. The slight financial relief which they might have obtained by frankly descending the social scale to live in the manner of the laboring classes was out of the question. It might have cost them their jobs.

A similar hidden pressure is put on the American white collar classes. It is mostly a matter of dress with the lesser clerks and typists. It extends to housing and cars and drinking parties as you go up the scale, and is intensified by the fact that for many jobs superficialities that "impress" people are nine-tenths of the qualifications. Advertising has been the major auxiliary to this situation.

Well, you can't have a car and a modern apartment, and wine with dinner and a Bendix and the "new look" and all the rest of it, and still have babies. Yet in our society these luxuries are not considered inordinate. We hope to have them for everybody. It is the American way of life. It is the "highest" standard of living in the world. It would not be possible were it not for contraception.

PALLIATIVES AND COMPROMISE

Efforts to resolve this dilemma work from both directions. Attempts to modify the Church's position center around "Rhythm." From the other direction, efforts at "social justice" are being made within the system.

"Rhythm" is a system of preventing conception by refraining from marital relations at certain times of the month. The Church permits it to be practiced under the advice of one's confessor because there are secondary purposes of sex which justify its unfruitful exercise when the unfruitfulness is nature's responsibility. The use of Rhythm without grave cause is sinful, but it is a different sin from that of artificial contraception. It is primarily a sin of selfishness. Nothing is so calculated to destroy the harmony of a marriage as selfishness, and Rhythm (used without cause) lets in just enough of it to destroy the orientation of the union, in preparation for the eventual release of the floodgates of self-seeking. In actuality, when Rhythm is so practiced it almost always leads to the use of artificial contraception.

Compromise from the other direction always has a nice sound when people talk about it. It aims at making a family possible within the present structure of society, and it centers its efforts around the "living wage." What is a living wage?

A living wage is enough to live on, and that obviously is a different amount for different people, depending on the size of one's family. In practice living wages are calculated on an arbitrary basis wherein a family is supposed to consist of a man and his wife and two children. If you have any more children, that's just too bad. If you are single, or married and without children, you benefit correspondingly. A living wage is not just. A family wage is what is needed, and that would involve paying men unequally for equal work. A little reflection will show that it would take a country full of saints for this equity to be effected. You just could not achieve it without abnormal virtue. It hasn't been tried here in the United States. In Europe it is the state which makes up the differences, a rather dangerous arrangement. So the injustice remains. The wage system offers a premium to the single and the childless, and a sort of martyrdom to those who follow the moral law.

BLESSINGS IN DISGUISE

Since the compromises won't work, there is only one way out of the dilemma for the modern couple. That is to hold firmly, with an heroic faith, to the moral standard of the Church, and, trusting in God's Providence, work to bring society and economics into line with that position. This sounds like sheer martyrdom, but maybe it is the gateway to a far better and fuller life. Actually, one can observe a sort of transformation taking place among the Catholic couples who have the courage to trust God. By the time the fifth child arrives they are completely out of harmony with modern society and they are thrown into a position where it is imperative for them to deepen their spiritual roots and shift over to living by Faith. Then they start building anew, at once for themselves and for society. They shed their bourgeois trappings, their superficial living habits, their selfishness, and the standards by which they formerly measured success. They usually move to the country, or to the outskirts of the city, and the men gradually manoeuvre themselves out of wage slavery into some far more interesting and apostolic work. Their former friends are left behind, with their vapid pleasures and decaying marriages, while the "unfortunate" couple is surrounded by their children "as olive branches round about their table"; and possessed of a mutual love infinitely remote from the possibility of divorce.

CHILDREN AND HOPE

Children are at once the symbol and personification of hope. They are the antidote, in a way, to the despair of modern society. With them comes a new energy, a new reason for perseverance. They are the material for which and through which a man and woman can lose themselves in love and so sanctify themselves.

Our world is like an aging, cynical financier, who spends his days calculating the awfulness and hopelessness of economics and politics, and his evenings in whatever revels his declining years and thinning pocketbook permit. If someone were to present him with a baby, aglow as babies are with freshness and innocence, a baby he couldn't get rid of, you would see a new vitality and reorientation in his life. Presently he would even abandon his doleful predictions and take to the streets to make things over personally.

·10·

Mirthless Pleasure

Few people have a good time any more. Though we are a nation of playboys and playgirls, though we have an entertainment industry that invades every village and town with its coast-to-coast broadcasts, its juke boxes and its double features, yet no one has any fun. The air is heavy, not light. Our laughter contains malice, or humorless acidity, or alcoholic unreason, or, very often, ribaldry. People dance, but without light hearts, or even light feet. They seldom sing. But they long for recreation, for pleasure and for leisure as seldom before. Why do men want so desperately to be amused? And why do they fail to find what they are seeking?

THE MERRY MIDDLE AGES

To solve our problem we must go back to the only time on earth when the atmosphere was pervaded by joy. It was the time when society was Catholic. Whatever may have been the shortcomings of the Middle Ages, they nevertheless were the ages of Faith. They were also the ages of Hope, and their keynote was joy. Merry England was Catholic England, and those who would confine it to the reign of Elizabeth (into which it overflowed, for the spirit of a people is a long time forming and a long time dying) will be at a loss to account for its origin.

Even today if we want to suggest merriment, as for example
on our Christmas card, we have to reproduce some medieval
scene. The sleighs, the colorful costumes, the roaring yule logs,
the great halls, the peasants making their way to Midnight
Mass—all hark back to the Middle Ages. There has been joy
since, but that was the only time when it characterized society.
The reason is not far to be sought. Joy is the overflow of hope,
and Christ brought hope into the world. So true is this that
you find no real joy anywhere except in Christianity. You find
other good things, such as nobility and beauty and courage and
love of truth in pagan societies at their best; you do not find
joy. Joy is the mark of Christianity. So wherever you find
Christianity which is not merely perfunctory, you find this
same joy. You find it in saints and other holy people, even in
the midst of suffering. You find it in deeply Catholic families.
You find it in religious communities, especially the contemplative orders. I remember walking by a convent of discalced
Carmelite nuns at recreation time. The people on the streets
around me looked weary and solemn and anxious, as always,
but from beyond the high wall came the gayest of childlike
laughter.

Where Christ is, joy is, but that is only here and there in
the modern world. In the Middle Ages it was pervasive. And
so at one medieval period there were 150 Holy Days, which
were also holidays, given to an overflow of joy. Celebrations
always centered around the church and the liturgy. The clothes
—but what have we today to compare with the holiday clothes
of the medieval peasants? There were processions, and dancing
and singing and contests. Everyone took part, whole family
units, whole parishes. Each feast day was different from the
others, as the liturgy constantly varies. Our modern theatre de-
rives from the plays which began on the altar and gradually
moved out of the church. Our modern parades are only a faint
echo of the processions which are (when you think of it) ad-
mirable focal points for any community celebration.

THE PURITAN PALL

The joy was taken out of life in one fell swoop by the Puritans, who represented the extreme of gloomy Calvinism. This is what an English writer has written about them and their continued effect on that England which was once known as merry.*

"(They) defaced the medieval churches, drove all the joy and beauty out of religion and frightened more people away from Christianity than any other body of people that ever lived. The Borgias were nothing to them. Under them we grew to mistrust the beauty of Catholic ceremony (so pagan), the graciousness of Catholic devotion (how decadent), and the delicacy of Catholic morals (how disingenuous). We learned to mistrust beauty and grace and tenderness and to believe it to be first a seduction, then a luxury. Even Catholics are not entirely free from it. In most people's minds there is a connection between piety and gloom, piety and ugliness, piety and the wet blanket. A cruder and saner age than ours (sometimes known as the Dark Ages) looked on sadness and despondency as a fault—even a sin. The Desert Fathers had a great deal of practical advice on combating *acedia*—or, in modern language, the blues. Now the spirit of gloom has disguised itself as love of the truth, that of phlegm as balance, mental laziness as humility, and you may reform the social order till you are black in the face, the next one bids fair to be as bad as this in time. For the shadow of the Puritans has settled down on us like a bad smell, and though we have outgrown their clothes the shadow and the smell remain behind."

When England could stand the Puritans and their gloom no longer she threw them out and they came to America, where they made New England their own. Their indirect influence still persists in other Protestant bodies. Wherever you find vio-

* C. M. Larkins in the September, 1947, *Integrity*.

lent prohibitionists, blue laws, and the forbidding of card playing on Sunday, you have the Puritan tradition lingering on. In their early days the Puritans tried to suppress Christmas because people were too merry on that occasion and merriment was not considered godly. It would be interesting to take a poll of ex-Protestants over fifty today. It would include many of our leading citizens, and I think it would be found that many of them ceased to practice religion when they became adult because of the horror of childhood Sundays spent in a Puritan gloom.

SECULARISM

Besides Puritanism there is another, and much worse, influence on modern recreational habits. It is now the prevailing influence and it is called secularism. Secularism separates religion from daily life, and has done a very thorough job in the matter of recreation. To it we owe the transformation from the religious procession and dancing in honor of the Saints, to Saturday night dinner-dancing at the modern luxury hotel.

Secularism really had its roots in the French Revolution, and from the very beginning severed the main ties which bind the ordinary men to the Church. It is interesting to consider one of them, the matter of Holy Days. If people make merry in honor of the mysteries of the Faith, or the birthdays of the Saints, the great truths of religion are kept before them and recreation naturally centers around the parish altar. Therefore, it is of great advantage to atheists to get rid of the Holy Days and substitute some other occasions for recreation. They did this as much as they were able at the French Revolution and they have been trying to finish the job ever since. That is why we celebrate the Fourth of July instead of Corpus Christi, the birthday of Abraham Lincoln instead of the Feast of St. Francis, and why Mother's Day is made more of in the papers than the Feast of the Immaculate Conception. We live in a

secularist's world and we work on Holy Days of obligation.
But no one has been able to get rid of Christmas and Easter.
And how they have tried! In Russia they have taken care to
force the people to work during the church hours on Christmas, and then had a public, atheistic celebration in the after-
noon, something like the dedication of a crematorium. In
Brooklyn they recently tried to forbid school children's singing
carols which mention the Nativity. Perhaps the department
stores have done even more to pervert the spirit of Christmas
in the United States. Yet it remains a unique feast in a post
Christian world, which touches the hearts of even the atheists,
which momentarily unites the subway herd in good-will and
fellowship, which makes drunkards remember God and business men open their hearts just a little. It is a faint whiff of
what a Christian society once was. No wonder Pius XI, in in-
stituting the Feast of Christ the King, pointed out how important liturgical feasts are for bringing home a realization of
Christianity to the popular mind. When the new Catholic
ferment gains strength in this country, one of its first aims will
be the fitting celebration of Holy Days.

Since secularism has long prevailed in our recreational habits
it will be well to examine some of the transformations it has
brought about.

1. As Holy Days formerly served to intensify the religious
spirit of the people, so secular holidays are auxiliary to the
worship of the state. You must celebrate something, and we do
celebrate significant events in the history of our nation. Who
can say that Bastille Day has not been partly responsible for
the almost fanatic love of France that you find in Frenchmen?
Or that the Fourth of July is not part of the idealization of the
United States? God is more important than the state and more
to be honored, but when public honor is given the state, and
not to God, which is going to seem more important in the public mind? Abraham Lincoln was a very noble man, but no
Saint Francis of Assisi, yet what relative importance would the

two be given by a public-school child? Since he will be inclined to emulate one or the other it is important that he see them in the right perspective.

2. The secularism of recreation has led to the commercialization of recreation. The church was the natural center of Christian merrymaking. Where will men seek pleasure now that they have broken with the parish? It has turned out that they will seek it wherever entertainment is provided for them, and over a period of time a new center has arisen to replace the church. It is the modern luxury hotel, which is, as Hitler pointed out, the symbol and center of modern bourgeois society. Not everyone goes to the local Ritz Plaza of a Saturday night, but that is the ideal of which the local tavern is the echo. It is now expensive to recreate, even if you go to the movies. This is a new note, too. There is no necessary connection between money and having a good time, but the two are almost inseparable in our day.

3. It isn't recreation alone that has changed. In the five hundred years or so since men rejoiced in their Christian hope there has been a progressive decline of religion, until men now suddenly wake up to realize that they are no longer Christians. Along with the de-Christianization of society has gone its mechanization and industrialization. What then is today's prevailing mood? It has completed the circuit away from the joy of hope. It is now at the opposite pole. The modern world is bathed in despair. Why then this frenzy of pleasure-seeking? How can it be the overflow of despair, as joy is the overflow of hope? Despair doesn't overflow. Its logical consequence is self-destruction. The present lust for pleasure is a gigantic effort to escape from despair. This is the essential reason for the perversion of recreation today. Men are striving for pleasure as never before, but in the wake of a relentless despair.

This is the genesis also of the cult of the leisure state. Men so detest their meaningless, monotonous jobs that they place all their hope in the escape after five o'clock and the mirage of the leisure state. This is not only the antithesis of the Christian thing but it is also the perversion of the nature of recreation. In the natural order, which Christ transformed, recreation is subordinate to work, and for the sake of work. You play so you can work better afterwards. Now we work only so we can play, and playing has become an end in itself, a sort of last-ditch beatitude.

4. It is because it is born of despair that our play is without pleasure. In the first place it is passive, and that is characteristic of despair too. Those who are without hope become heavy and inert, incapable of initiative and vitality. They are just the sort to sit hours every night in a movie house, or spend Saturday afternoons on the bleachers, or days drugged beside the radio. And they are so obviously without joy. One needs only to visit the nearest bar in order to be thoroughly depressed by men and women for whom drinking is a grim and earnest business. Their only gaiety is alcohol-induced. Night clubs are a nightmare of forced hilarity. In some of them one senses a terrifying foretaste of Hell. Walk down the streets in the amusement center of any city and ignore, for once, the lights and the noise. Study instead the faces of the people, especially of the women. You will be frightened by the absence of joy in the marts of joy of the modern world.

THE DATING SYSTEM

The dating system needs special treatment, because dates are not merely a form of recreation, but more importantly constitute our system of pairing off the race for the purposes of matrimony.

I think it can be said without qualification that of all the systems that have ever been devised for young men and young women to meet and mate, the dating system is the worst. In some South American towns it is the custom on Sundays for the young men and young women to form concentric circles

and walk around in opposite directions for the purpose of eye-
ing one another. However absurd this may seem, it is far more
intelligent than the dating system, which has, as far as one can
determine, absolutely nothing to recommend it.

The problem regarding the young is this: there should be
some way for them to meet a number of suitable prospective
mates, on a casual but natural basis, without there being any
danger of their hearts becoming prematurely involved. This
preliminary period should be followed by the courtship during
which the two should have ample opportunity to get to know
each other, with a reasonable amount of precaution taken
against too great intimacy. Our dating system covers the whole
process. It is expected to provide first of all a means of meeting,
people of the opposite sex, but it is in itself a means of meeting
no one. It is an initial pairing off before there is any occasion
for pairing off. Theoretically, you ought not to go out on a
date before you are old enough to get married or with anyone
you are certain not to want to marry. However, in practice this
is impossible because our society provides no other means of
recreation, so the date has to serve as general recreation as well
as a marriage bureau. Furthermore, although dates isolate people in pairs they nevertheless hold out the only hope for ever
getting into things and meeting (it will always be more or less
by chance) someone else who might be suitable to marry. So
young people are more or less forced to go out on dates habitu-
ally, and this need carries with it many dangers. The most
obvious is the threat to purity which the date presents of its
very nature. Or again, there is the danger of marrying un-
wisely merely because two people are thrown together so often
that physical attraction makes them seem suited when really
they are not. But supposing purity is possible in particular
cases, it still is harmful to go on dates with any sort of regularity. A girl will come to her marriage less fresh for having
exerted herself to entertain a succession of men over a period
of years. Indeed men sense this and are reluctant to marry girls

who have dated for too long. On the other hand a man who has dated for a long time is likely to have turned into the eternal playboy. Men have a hard enough time maturing these days without spending ten or fifteen years on the preliminaries to the preliminaries to marriage, on the superficialities of friendships which have no reason to exist on that level, and cannot safely deepen.

One last ironic result of dating is that for all the years spent in dating the pair rarely if ever see each other in normal circumstances. The locus of the date is the movie theatre, the dance floor and the automobile. All that most girls know about their boy friends is whether or not they dance well, a fact of absolutely no importance matrimonially. The home life of the date, which can be so revealing of character, is the hidden life of the date. No one who really understands the dating system ought to wonder at our divorce rate.

THE FALSE REFORM

Many good people, desiring to see recreation again centered around the church, and not recognizing the essential perversion that has taken place in its nature, are attempting to mend the breach by church sponsorship of secular recreation. Dances are held in parish halls, on Saturday nights of course, because modern dancing (complete with juke box) has been taken over bodily, and naturally is not related to the liturgy, nor can be. I know of a man who sent his daughter away to school just so she would not be able to attend CYO dances, which were held in local hotels without chaperonage, in semi-dark rooms, to semi-erotic music.

Indeed, owing to secularism, the church has been robbed of so many of its community functions that the church organizations have gone overboard to recapture at least the physical presence of the youth in the proximity of the church whether by sports or dances. There is no need to enlarge on the theme.

Some church organizations have concentrated so much on entertainment that they have become spiritually and intellectually impotent. Most of them now realize it and are making an effort to deepen the spiritual roots of the organizations. It is up-hill work, because the membership has been attracted by the lure of pleasure.

THE NATURE OF THE REAL REFORM

There is no possibility of remedying our recreational distortion on the superficial level, by brightening the lights or being a little discriminating about the music or anything of that sort. There is neither any permanent possibility of reform on what you might call the *natural* level, although something can be done here to substitute the wholesome for the jaded, the healthy for the erotic. For instance, folk dancing is good on the natural level. It would be a suitable vehicle for Christian recreation (in fact it was) and a welcome change from the pairing off of modern dancing and dating. At present it serves the American Communists as a ground for recreation and proselytization, the heavy-drinking suburban pagans as an occasional novelty, as well as radical Catholic groups who have begun to realize the unwholesome nature of the modern dance. But folk dancing will not in itself make anything *Christian*, because Christianity has to do with Christ and not just with naturally good things.

The real reform in recreation awaits a changed direction in men's lives. It will involve a turning away from the lust for pleasure to an intensity of work for Christ. It will involve giving men hope to woo them from their despair, which means a hope in Christ. Then there will be everything important to do. When Catholics begin to realize the great work of the apostolate that is going to be done in our day, then it will be as though a new life has entered them, and twenty-four hours will not be a long enough day to spend restoring all things in Christ.

Wherever there are cells of Catholic Action or centers of

other genuine apostolic activity, young people have lost all track of the movies and haven't time to listen to the radio, or sit in a baseball bleachers. They cease to go out on dates, but meet ten times as many young people of the opposite sex in the course of their apostolic activities, and meet them at prayer and in discussions and in groups. In the midst of all the work, and out of the liturgy (the pilgrimages, the celebration of feast days, the study weeks) the hope of Christ begins to overflow in joy again and naturally gives rise to a new Christian recreation. There are feasts and picnics and processions and plays. There are nights spent in discussion, and long remembered. There are even special celebrations and feasts celebrated by apostles who are imprisoned in Europe, out of a gift package shared all around. There are even Communion breakfasts of a new sort, not expensive, formal affairs held in the leading hotel, but simple, informal, joyful breakfasts like the agape of old. The progress of the apostolate is the measure of the distance which lies between the mirthless present and Merry America.

·11·

Secularism

SEPARATION of religion from life is the basic perversity of our age. Its technical name is secularism. The bishops of the United States have declared it to be the root evil of our day, yet we scarcely notice it because, like the air we breathe, it is omnipresent. An analogy might help us to see what secularism really is.

Let us imagine a very large house (the world) in which there are a myriad of children (us) in the care of their mother (religion, God, or the Church, variously). As in all households full of children, things run more or less smoothly, the children behaving now better, now worse, and not infrequently fighting with each other.

At a certain point in the history of this household, vicissitudes of a new and disturbing nature occur. They aren't of the order of more or less troublesome, they are in the order of a direct attack on the organizational structure of the household, and often wear the exterior guise of angelic behavior. Let us trace some of these happenings.

As a pervasive undercurrent is the progressive neglect of the children to acknowledge, and finally even to realize, that they *are* children, and that their mother stands in a maternal relationship to them. They begin to take their existence for granted, being too preoccupied with their toys, busy exploring the house

G

or concentrated on stealing possessions from one another, to worry about origins. A few, who like to know where they come from or where they are headed for, try to think up the reasons all by themselves. They bandage their eyes (lest they see Mother) and sit in a corner of a dark room, thinking. Some of them decide that because they can't imagine how children could have come to be, the mystery is unfathomable. Others, whose presumption is of a slightly different variety, proclaim that children are the haphazard result of a chance meeting of elements, or that they have gradually developed from household pets. If and when these children (the philosophers, as they are called) speak of Mother it is as though she were infinitely remote and irrelevant. It doesn't occur to any of them to seek her out and learn from her.

Naturally children with a growing disdain for their parent are anything but obedient. Some of them broke with Mother's authority hundreds of years ago in a revolt euphemistically called a reformation. Other children assayed a somewhat different type of rebellion which they called an enlightenment, which meant they were too proud to accept Mother's authority. Multitudes of children have subsequently gone their own way through weakness or self-indulgence.

In proportion as the disobedience grew, so did the children's quarrels with one another. Unlike the former fights, these new ones seemed never really to stop, there being no recognized authority to whom both warring elements could appeal for arbitration. By now the fights involve the whole household and are almost without respite. Hatred and mistrust are everywhere.

A further unfortunate result of filial disobedience is the loss of objective and absolute rules of conduct. It has almost got so now that each child makes up his own rules for right or wrong. The results can be imagined.

SECULAR EDUCATION

When the children first decided Mother wasn't necessary in the classroom it didn't look as though the results would be as disastrous as they have now proved to be. They merely dispensed with a course called "Religion," in which the children had been taught about Mother and Mother's rules, information which at the time they could readily get elsewhere. The other courses were much the same as formerly. The children had been so long under Mother's care that they thought her fundamental rules were part of their natural endowment and didn't need special teaching. It turned out, however, that the schools the children set up were strong only in proportion as the children remembered Mother's principles. They had a tacit agreement that nothing would be taught in the common classroom that wasn't commonly accepted, so as time went on one fundamental principle after another disappeared from general consensus, and therefore from the classroom. Presently nothing was taught except "facts," which is to say only events and things that can be seen and measured. Woe to the teacher-child who interpreted or speculated. Student-children were crawling all over the house, measuring and counting and specifying and observing, but they didn't know the *meaning* of anything.

"This is a door," one of the teachers would say.

If there were a student so rash as to ask: "And what is the significance of doors?" he would likely get an answer like this:

"In the days of Mother they used to say that doors had to do with going in and out, but we don't want to be dogmatic, and truthfully, we don't know what the significance of doors is. However, I understand there is going to be a committee formed of eminent door-specialists who are going to make a comprehensive study of 3,000 doors to see if they can discover their significance, or at least to correlate their findings with the window research committee to see if there is any significant relationship between the incidence of doors and the incidence of windows in the third floor southern wing of the house."

But we are going ahead of our story. You see, finally the studies became absolutely devoid of principle or significance, and that turned out to be an intolerable situation. Student children began to sicken of learning that John went from the dining room to the attic 150 years ago, or that the three-year-olds fought the four-year-olds for ten years, without getting any explanation for either event. It was found that graduate children applying for positions only knew such things as, say, "the amount of dirt which accumulates over a week's period in summer on the third slat of the venetian blind on the second window of the third attic bedroom." All the educated children were very unhappy and completely disoriented. Quite a number of them went insane or dropped intellectual pleasures for those of the flesh, or turned, as they called it, "anti-social."

As we approach the present-day classroom situation we find principles and significance creeping in again, but different ones. These are derived from the learned studies of the window experts and the door experts, derived from seeing and measuring; statistics interpreted in the light of personal prejudice. They have nothing to do with Mother and her principles. But the old religion course no longer leaves a void. It is being replaced by a secular equivalent called "Mental Hygiene," which purports to help students lead "meaningful" lives in a household which has forgotten its meaning.

RELIGION IS A PRIVATE AFFAIR

Where has Mother been all this time? She's been relegated to the kitchen. The children put her there at the time they invented tolerance. They said it wasn't right for her to be around the house but that anyone could go out in the kitchen to see her who wanted to. Quite a few children did go out to see her, and still do. Even those who do go out now think the kitchen is the normal place for Mother to be, and that she has no real place in the children's social life, play or study. Those who know Mother have special private, "inside" feelings for when they are out in the kitchen, but otherwise you can hardly distinguish them from the rest of the children.

After Mother was confined to the kitchen it was considered slightly indecent to talk about her in ordinary conversation. In inverse proportion as Mother was not talked about the children started speaking of the things Mother had formerly forbidden them to mention publicly, as indecent.

Once Mother was relegated to the kitchen her picture and personal effects disappeared too. Formerly in a tour of the house you were constantly reminded of Mother and her goodness, but nowadays if you walk through the rooms you are only reminded of what the children are trying to sell one another.

Almost completely absent also is Mother's birthday, along with the birthdays of her favorite children. They had to go, of course, if Mother was to be got rid of. Deprived of their Holy Days, the children insisted on some holidays, so a few were invented. Almost every corner of the house had been tyrannized at one time or another by the local bully, who was eventually overthrown. A series of Independence Days arose as occasions for picnics, parades and fireworks. Also you will find a sprinkling of Armistice Days to mark attempts at peace which have since proved failures. The children also celebrate the birthdays of local political and military heroes, whose glorious and not so glorious deeds are virtually obsolete. These secular holidays serve to give the younger children a vague worship of political government and an unreasoned loyalty to their particular corners of the house. This will be useful to future tyrants.

MOTHERS ARE THE MORPHINE OF THE PEOPLE

Every now and again one of the children gets sick and howls for his Mother. When this happens some of the other children are disdainful and spread it abroad that only weaklings need mothers. They have invented a slogan, which goes like this: "Mothers are the morphine of the people." Some of the children who used to sneak out in the kitchen to see Mother have stopped now because they are ashamed of being considered weaklings.

Meanwhile Mother, who seems infinitely patient, continues to keep the house going. She cooks and heals and patches, even though the children pretend she doesn't. Formerly Mother used to preside over the dinner table and the children, knowing she had provided the food, used to turn to her before beginning to eat, and said "Thank you, Mother." They called this "saying grace." All the food still comes from Mother, but circuitously and precariously, owing to the many quarrels and the amount of greed that now exists among the children. The child who puts it on the table has it from a child who has wrapped and packaged it, who has it from a child who has run around the house with it twice, who has it from a child who has pressed or stamped or dehydrated it, who has it from a child who went to the kitchen door and got it from Mother. This complicated process is known as the economic system, and the children often congratulate each other on having it, saying, "If we hadn't invented so clever a system, we wouldn't be able to eat."

THE FAILURE OF SECULARISM

It has finally come to the point where all the children in our house are involved in a fight that is threatening to pull the house down around their shoulders, and they are quite unable to make peace. They cannot even make a bad peace or a temporary peace. All the things that caused the wars and made them horrible continue to develop by a relentless logic of their own: the mutual hate and suspicion because of which each child is isolated and afraid, the rapid transportation and instantaneous communication which aggravate these enmities, the clever inventions of the clever children for their mutual destruction, the greedy cornering of the necessities of life in disregard of the common good.

Not only the main fight, but all the little quarrels within quarrels are rooted in the unnatural separation of Mother from her parental rôle. Hardly anyone realizes this. Wandering through the house you frequently find children quarreling, as for example, thus:

"I want $100 a week!"

"I can't afford to give you $100 a week!"

If you were to admonish these children by saying, "Now, boys, didn't Mother tell you both not to be greedy?" they would only look at you in amazement and dismay.

"*What*," they would ask, "has Mother to do with this?" And they would produce a roomful of detailed data *in re* the particulars and history of their quarrel. Everything would be there except the main fact, that they are self-seeking in a situation which calls for self-sacrifice.

Well, that is secularism. We are the children, we Catholics, who sneak out in the kitchen to see Mother. We are the bridge between the world's problems and troubles (in which we ourselves are involved), and the Church which has the grace and truth to solve these problems and save the children. We (especially Catholic *lay* people) are the key to the solution, and that is why there has been so much talk about lay initiative and responsibility in the modern Church. Obviously (we have but to look around) we are not better, braver, more talented, wiser, or even of better will, than our non-Catholic friends. It is just that we happen (mostly by accident of birth) to be the connecting link between a troubled world and the fullness of truth and love. What we are ill-fitted for by nature, God will fit us for by grace if we will consent to be His instruments.

Our outstanding mark must be apostolicity. It is always one of the marks of the Church, but today it is the great mark of spiritual health among lay people. If we children sneak out into the kitchen for our own consolation and afterwards turn aside from the sorrows and confusions of our brothers and sisters, what is to be said of our charity, which is the mark of holiness? In even worse conscience will be those lay Catholics who in a tormented world are looking to their own "security." Seeking security today is like trying to find some remote corner of our imaginary house, there to hide from all responsibility. Or it is to hoard a large share of necessities against one's starving brother's needs. It is wholly unfitting and degrading for a Catholic.

We must bring our brothers and sisters two things: truth and love. In respect of truth we must show them that all their problems are basically spiritual problems to which moral and spiritual principles must be applied. This is essentially an intellectual job; that of knowing the faith thoroughly, seeing the world for what it is, and putting the two together.

Bringing love and unity to a world in hatred and isolation will be like bringing a flaming torch into a cold and cheerless room. The only love we can bring is supernatural charity, God's love; and the condition of our carrying it to our brothers and sisters is that we first be ignited by it ourselves. Quite simply, we must be saints. Then men will say "See those Christians, how they love one another," and go seeking the source of our strength. That will mark the end of secularism, and the beginning of the reign of Christ the King.

·12·

Machine *versus* Hand Facture

T HE ROOT economic fight today is not capital versus labor, it is the machine tenders versus the machine smashers. It is not primarily an economic problem, as I hope to show, but it is the economic aspect of a spiritual problem. Still, it can be examined on the economic plane. Shall we smash the big machines which have changed our whole way of making things? (More likely we shall be smashed by them.) Or shall we let them do our work for us? It is the argument of the craftsman versus Number 32 on the assembly line; the musician versus the man who dials the radio; the artist versus the automaton; the creator versus the comfort seeker. It is *not* an argument between the primitive and the man of progress, as it is often represented. Rather it is the quarrel between culture and the new barbarianism. The machine smasher esteems tools that add to the dexterity of his hand, whether the lathe or the surgeon's instrument. The machines which replace his intellect and skill are the ones he loathes.

Just at present the American public is all-out in admiration of machines and the assembly line. Hardly anyone will even argue the matter. We like the machine age, and even if we don't, we see that it is all-pervasive and seemingly here to stay. We ought to take a sharp look at the two places where crafts still flourish in America. One is among the rich and the other is among the insane. That's really very significant. The people who can afford to have their clothes, cars, art work, shoes and dresses made any way they want, choose craftsmanship. They think that custom-made clothes are better than ready-made; that Rolls-Royces are better cars than Nashes, etc. The very people who have fatted on mass manufacture for *us*, decline to patronize it themselves. Now consider the insane. They *do* crafts. It's supposed to soothe them and help them recover their sanity. If this is the case, then the worker whose work no longer has anything in common with craft work has lost a major weapon against his own mental disintegration. All reports confirm this.

Furthermore, certain glaring ills of society can be laid directly, in the economic order, to machine facture. They are not little diseases, they are monstrous plagues on the social order. It would be well to consider a few of them.

LOSS OF FREEDOM

Certain it is that modern man has lost his independence, and certain it is that this can be laid at the door of machine facture. The question is no longer slavery or freedom. We are all slaves. Only a few men really control their own economic destinies, as formerly did the craftsman and small farmer. The question is only whether our slavery will be comfortable or not, profitable or not. Belloc clearly showed our loss of freedom in *The Servile State*, written twenty or thirty years ago and recently re-published. The more enslaved we are economically, the more we pride ourselves on our political freedom, such as it is. Anyhow, as Belloc says, the right to vote is a pretty empty liberty in the absence of property ownership and economic independence. No one dares say this openly now, but universal franchise has been traced to industrialization, the thesis being that, when men's economic freedom was wrested from them they were given the vote as a solace, and made to feel that freedom had been restored, although it was really only a semblance of freedom.

THE LEISURE STATE

The second noticeable result of machine facture is that men no longer like to work. Everything evidences this. Men no longer sing at work, but they once did. No folk music has come from the Pennsylvania coal mines or the Detroit factories. Modern work is a grim business, to be endured.

Another sign that men don't like to work is that they have such a mania for money. Jobs are measured by salaries, and scarcely talked about in any other terms. This avarice is not without provocation. Most men are not naturally avaricious, only a few. That the generality of men has fallen so low must be because it is the only incentive to work. Occasionally one meets someone who wants an *interesting* job, but most people know already that jobs aren't interesting in a machine age.

Still another measure of the unrest and discontent abroad about jobs is seen in the universality of the ideal of the leisure state. We shall work less and less, men say to themselves, and we shall play more and more. And so they have done until now. With wars and rumors of wars, the attainment of the leisure state is postponed, but men do not cease to long for it. Comfort and leisure are what men dream of and work for. But this would not be the case if their work were interesting and creative, as is craft work. Then they would more easily turn their thoughts to doing *good* work, and stop watching the clock.

MEN WHO NEVER GROW UP

Insane asylums know that crafts develop a man, in virtue and skill and in all sorts of subtle ways. Many a lesson in the spiritual life is learned almost unconsciously by hand work. A man knows what it is to go with the grain of a task or a person after he has worked intimately with the grain of wood. He knows what Catholic Action means about leavening from having made leavened bread. He knows a lot about faults and sins from weeding. It is through work that is really creative and responsible and that needs skill that a man develops into a man. If you take responsibility away from him, if you do not let him develop his mind or his talents, if you do not give him something to think about, he is far less a man than he would have been. He will probably become neurotic. He will very likely fall from virtue. He will be a broken and corrupted and essentially useless member of society.

Even if you don't like men manly or strong or intelligent, you will want them to save their souls and practice virtue. This is extremely hard for modern man. He has to release his energy somehow, and the somehow is coming by common consent to be sex or liquor. Quite apart from these gross lapses, it is noticeable that one seldom meets a man (or woman) who is really *whole*, much less holy, who understands and has disciplined himself. Where will he learn virtue? Against what will he try himself? Take the matter of patience. The practice of the virtue of patience is integral to hand facture, whether it be in sewing or making shoes or carving statues. You can only go just so fast and you have to allow for the nature of the material on which you are working. But patience in the machine age consists mostly (and more and more) in standing in line waiting for something, whether to get in the subway, or collect your pay envelope, or get in the movies. In England "queuing," as they call it, occupies a major part of every citizen's life. Now a different sort of patience is required for this sort of thing than for making things. One is constantly tempted to anger, feeling perpetually frustrated and bitter at the inefficiency of the thing. In his heart everyone feels that all this waiting is unnecessary, and one needs to be a saint to put up with unnecessary and stupid delays, or else one becomes resigned, which is a different thing from patience. The ordinary man can learn fairly easily to be patient with natural waits. No one feels frustrated in July because it isn't Christmas yet, or gets angry about snow because it takes time to melt.

So the modern machine age man is without a suitable school of virtue. The result is that he is characteristically immature and undeveloped, especially undeveloped spiritually. This has repercussions everywhere, and one of them is that people today are having nervous and mental breakdowns at an unprecedented rate.

WASTE

The machine age wastes on a prodigious scale. It wastes time (carting things around the world and back again; substituting systems for initiative). It wastes natural resources, of course. If God allows us to continue in this direction much longer, there won't be any coal or wood or oil or fertility of soil left in the world. The machine age wastes wealth too, wealth of all kinds. It wastes Mr. Smith's salary and Brazilian coffee and United States wheat. It makes things deliberately of poor grade, and changes fashions so women will throw away their clothes, and pours millions of dollars into correcting the ills it has engendered. It wastes effort too. It takes men from primary production and busies them selling or advertising or carrying things here and there or planning. More and more people are being absorbed (perhaps one ought to say entrapped) in bureaucracies, becoming parts of vast systems, stupid, routine parts. It is interesting to note how this works. There is a company which makes business machines to replace responsible human work. These machines, when patiently tended, do things like make out the payrolls of companies. But if one of these machine monsters is rented by a company having a payroll personnel of, say, twenty-five people, when they will need no longer twenty-five but twenty-seven people. Of course, the machine will be doing all the intelligent work. The twenty-seven people will be feeding the machine mechanized information and (mostly) correcting the errors which result from feeding it wrong information because the job is too dull to keep their minds on it.

HERE IT IS

Well, the machine age, for all these major disorders, and others besides, is here to stay, so its champions insist. There must be something good about it. What? They would have a list like this: automobiles, washing machines, prepared and adulterated foods, atom bombs, airplanes, radios, sky-scrapers, etc.

But are all these so wonderful? Some of them are bad per se, like the atom bomb. Some are marvelous (in the literal sense) but silly—like skyscrapers. Most are contingent things. Radios are useful if you have something to say and no other means of communicating it. Automobiles are useful if you aren't already where you want to be. (Religious sometimes take a vow of stability. There must be some spiritual benefit to be derived from finding a good place and staying there.) Airplanes are useful under the same conditions, and providing that the pilots and mechanics are skilled and conscientious. Yet other things are handy (like the Bendix) but not worth the sacrifice of sanctity, domestic felicity, or political peace.

Along with them go congestion, commuting, time clocks, advertising, women in industry, ugliness everywhere, the destruction of nature, the loss of the home as an economic unit, materialism and an incalculable cost in souls.

Who can say that all has come to stay and be resigned to it?

THE TAIL END OF THE CRAFTS

Although machines have dominated our culture for some time, there were always a few craftsmen left, or at least a tradition of craftsmanship. Men still learned to navigate by the stars, even though they expected to navigate by radio. It is just in our day that the thing has finally come to an end.

Now one finds that only old printers know how to set type by hand, only old dressmakers know how to sew well (where good seamstresses are in demand, as in the alterations department of dress shops, almost all the women will be the other side of fifty, and no young girls are undertaking apprenticeship). The silversmiths in Sheffield, England, are dying out. Here in America the men in building trades who could build a simple house, for instance, are old men. The young workers do their own specialty and would be helpless to undertake a job calling for a variety of related skills. Housewives cannot make bread and soon will forget how to wash clothes; their culinary ability is being narrowed down to heating up things. The evening before an annual financial report was due in a publishing house the adding machine broke. As a result the editor stayed up all night making the report, because he was the only member of the firm old enough to know how to add. During the war one of the bright mass-circulation magazines sent an editorial writer around to gather material for a feature article on the ten most wonderful machines here in America. She visited all the large factories and asked "What's the most remarkable machine you have here?" The article was never written. It turned out that the ten most remarkable machines were hand-made in Germany.

THE POST-ATOMIC AGE

The machine tenders have put us in a worse state than they imagined. They have rendered us impotent to fend for ourselves in this world, furnishing us instead with everything ready-made, prepared, ready to serve, simplified to the turn of a dial. They then invented the atom bomb, which could, within several hours, destroy the whole, hopelessly interdependent system and put us right back into simple savagery. And it would be savagery. No one would know anything—how to build a house, or weave a garment, or make bread, or fashion shoes, or tell a story. We would become barbarians overnight because we are barbarians already.

ALL ROOT PROBLEMS ARE SPIRITUAL

So it really isn't an economic problem after all. The machine tenders are destroying themselves and us—and this more or less against their will. The machine smashers have lost their battle long since and are now moth-eaten and nearly extinct. There is nothing to choose between them. We do really have the machines for this little, delirious, nightmarish time that remains before night closes in on Western civilization. The only solution is in the religious order. There is only one thing that can dignify man now, whether he be a distorted old craftsman, or a young factory animal, whether he can still go to Radio City, or is wandering around the ruins of New York, or the cheap shabbiness of a cultureless Midwestern town suddenly thrown on its own nothingness—cut off from Hollywood and the National Broadcasting Company, from Quaker Oats, "My Sin" perfume, and frozen foods in unseasonal variety. One day, please God, modern man will fall on his knees, and then he will see the horrible noise and complexity and superficiality and luxury of our day for what it is. If he sees and repents soon enough, he may be able to save some of the present structure to use in building a new world.

·13·

The Animal Synthesis

I<small>N THIS</small> book we have tried to show the subtle nature of today's problems. Ours is a world in which most of the harm is being done by men of good will who are not also men of good sense. Evil masquerades as good as never before, while the multitudes are so estranged from the fundamentals of living and profundity of thought, that they are deceived on every hand. And, indeed, it is not easy to see through the welter of deception. Perhaps it will help clarify things to show that all these separate evils operate on the same general principle and are converging into a synthesis of evil in which each plays a functional part.

In the Middle Ages we came near to having a Christian synthesis of life and institutions, in which every action of a man's life was meaningful in relation to Christ. Whether he blessed his bread, joined his guild, danced on a Holy Day or married a wife, the medieval man was a Christian and all these actions had meaning in respect to his Christianity.

Today a similar thing is happening. We are fast moving into a synthesis of life, but away from Christ. It is not enough to see this or that evil in isolation. We must see the pattern that is being formed.

H

THE KEY PRINCIPLE

The orientation of life today is not so much anti-Christianity as mock-Christianity. We do not oppose charity with hate, but with philanthropy; freedom with slavery (at least ostensibly), but with license. We do not dignify man as another Christ, but as a substitute for God. What we cherish today is the analogously good, *that which looks like the real thing, but is in a lower order.* We are making a synthesis around man the mere animal instead of around man raised to share God's life. Let us call it the animal synthesis. You can see this basic principle running through all of modern life. What is happening is not simply that man is being treated badly, but that man is being treated like an animal. Sometimes he is treated very kindly, but when he is, it is with the sort of kindness and pity and mercy fitted for a dog or a horse or a cow, but not for Christ's brothers.

Let us examine a few of the areas in which the animal synthesis is forming.

THE SELECTIVE BREEDING OF HUMAN BEINGS

A farmer has a certain control over the rate of reproduction of his farm animals. If he wants a lot of chickens or cows or pigs, he breeds them as fast as nature will allow, and without, of course, any concern for monogamy among the stock. One rooster may become the father of hundreds of chickens, one bull sire several generations of calves from many different cows. Hitler, Mussolini and Stalin must have thought of themselves as like the farmer, free to forcebreed citizens for gun fodder or other utilitarian purposes. At any rate they encouraged human breeding as fast as nature would allow, and in disregard of God's regulations in the matter. God, Whose decision it really ought to be, has said to us "increase and multiply," but not at random; within marriage. In America we do not encourage illegitimate births, but we too try to regulate the number of us, only in the other direction. We are like the farmer who wants to hold down his animals to a convenient number. She-dogs and cats are liable to be deprived of their fertility right away. We have the same idea in respect to some of the innocents among us, who might inconvenience us (and cost us money) by reproducing. A farmer "spaces" his calves so that his cows will be fresh in alternation and at his convenience. We've adopted that idea in our planned parenthood organizations. Unlike the farmer, though, we have not been able to establish any objective criterion for the spacing interval. At first it was thought that a couple should synchronize their reproduction rate with their income, but incomes are unstable, liable to change, and useless as criteria without reference to the standard of living. Now, in fact, it happened that the rich and educated wouldn't have enough babies and the poor persisted in having an excessive number, so that economics fell by the wayside as a criterion. Then we tried health, but it was impossible to establish the fact that having babies in regular succession was unhealthy. There remains no standard except the caprice (or selfishness) of the couple. It is as though the cows themselves regulated their reproduction, for we are no more made for ourselves than they are made for themselves.

Let us return to our farmer. It sometimes suits his convenience to breed his cows with bulls at a distance. He has perfected a method of artificial insemination to accomplish his purpose, and this method has recently been adopted by human beings as a way of siring babies where natural methods fail or are inadvisable. Many legal and moral problems arise from this new practice, which sprang into use without much preliminary testing, since it had already been perfected in animal husbandry.

CONDITIONING HUMAN BEINGS FOR PRODUCTION

Since animals exist for the sake of men, it is legitimate to put them to work and force them, within limits, to a certain quantity and rhythm of production. You can whip a horse or saddle or harness him, put a yoke on oxen, feed up pigs for the market, give cows a productive diet, and even (although it seems wrong and probably is) keep the lights on in the chicken coop to trick the hens into laying more eggs.

Men have to work too, but they have free wills and so should have a certain autonomy of operation in their labors. The best guarantee of their freedom is the widespread private ownership of productive property, a condition which is now only a remote memory or an almost impossible dream. The vast majority of men are wage earners in huge impersonal enterprises where they are subjected to animal-like conditions of labor. They are not (yet) whipped into physical effort here, as they are in Russia. Machines furnish most of the necessary power. The modern worker's labor takes less strength than formerly, but is more subtly corroding.

The assembly line offends man's human dignity in several ways. For one thing it determines arbitrarily and irresistibly the rhythm of his work. A free man varies the speed of his work and rests at irregular intervals. It is also true that one man's natural rhythm of work is not another man's. The assembly belt standardizes them all, the plodders and the men who want to work in spurts and the speed demons, so that no one is really satisfied, and everyone is made nervous by the unvarying regularity of the thing. Furthermore, the monotony is killing, this having one little, often meaningless, bit to contribute to a remote whole. That wouldn't bother animals. You can even harness them to a treadmill if you put blinders on them to keep their attention from wandering. But if you put blinders on men, there will nevertheless be revolts and distractions and unhealthy ideas generated from within, which in time will sicken the whole.

There are various ways of forcing men to subhuman work. One is stark, economic necessity such as faces the propertyless man. That worked for a long time until men realized that they had a collective power of bargaining if they organized in trade unions. Then was their golden opportunity of escaping to a more human life, but this time they were bought off by the actuality of high wages and the promise of a succession of luxuries instead of the necessities of space and air and houses and children and human, responsible work. By now most of their power of revolt has vanished and they are docile, if unhappy, cogs in the wheels of industry. Sheer boredom and indifference now make their work lethargic and inaccurate.

Interesting in this connection is the use of Musak, canned music with which offices and factories are experimenting. At first glance, music while you work sounds like a fine idea. If you stretch your imagination you can even compare it with the milking songs and harvest songs of a former age. Here is another case where something looks like the real thing but is worlds apart. The folk music of old grew up spontaneously from the workers themselves, as an expression of their joy or their community spirit, or to set a rhythm for common work which needed coordination. Musak bears more resemblance to the conditioning of guinea pigs in traps. It starts with an unhappy mass of mechanical workers who have neither initiative nor responsibility nor liking in their jobs and who persistently fall into a lethargy. Personnel men have found that music can stimulate these human robots to quicker production by working directly through their senses, almost as though they had no brains at all.

Anything that interferes with production is anathema to personnel men and factory owners. The moral law as such means nothing to them. That is how it comes about that adultery and the telling of dirty jokes is generally tolerated in

offices and factories (unless there be scandal attached) whereas
talking about religion is frowned upon. In one large insurance
company some Catholic Action girls were asked to refrain from
saying grace in the company's lunch room. Rightly too, according to the philosophy of these slave establishments. The personnel department must have sensed that public acknowledge-
ment of God was harking back rather dangerously to the
human.

DOCTORS TURNING VETERINARIANS

Euthanasia is among the most clear-cut manifestations of the
new animal synthesis.

If man has an immortal soul and is destined for eternal life,
then this world is thrown in perspective. It becomes a trying
ground and a path to eternal life. Even suffering has its place,
and even mental defectives have their function. God's ways
are inscrutable at times, but we have no right to take our own
lives or the lives of innocent fellow citizens, no matter whether
or not it seems to us that death would be a blessing. We are
made by God and for God. He alone knows when our time
should be up.

On the other hand, animals exist for us. Within certain
limits we can do what we want with them. We have over them
the power of life and death. If a cat has too many kittens (for
our convenience) we can drown a litter. If a dog is mortally
wounded we can "put him out of his misery." There is no
after-life for dogs which would make their sufferings meritori-
ous. But that is not true of our cancerous Aunt Kate, the meaning of whose suffering is known to God Who has permitted it.
The pity of the mercy-killers is like the pity we have for suffering animals. It rests on a dogmatic disbelief in the higher life
and immortality. It therefore is certain that no possible good
can come from suffering. What is amazing is not that the modern pagans should have fallen into this error, and sentimen-

tality, but that expressed Christians should make it so explicit. Several hundred Protestant and Jewish clergymen recently made the following astonishing public statement:

> We no longer believe that God wills the prolongation of physical torture for the benefit of the soul of the sufferer. For one enduring continual and severe pain from an incurable disease, who is a burden to himself and his family, surely life has no value.
>
> We believe that such a sufferer has the right to die, and that society should grant this right, showing the same mercy to human beings as to the sub-human animal kingdom. "Blessed are the merciful."

PROFESSOR KINSEY

We are indebted to Professor Kinsey for making explicit a principle which has long been implicit in modern teaching on sex. When Professor Kinsey was asked, a propos of his book, *The Sexual Behavior in the Human Male*, how he found it possible to maintain an amoral view of impurities and perversions, he said, "Man is a mammal, and I therefore take my standards from the mammals."

That expresses in brief the whole modern position in respect to sex and marriage. Man is made, not in the image and likeness of God, but in the image and likeness of animals. It follows that marriage is like the mating of animals. Neither purity nor fidelity nor monogamy is relevant.

The Christian view of marriage is that it resembles the union of Christ and His Church. It is not even so much a natural institution as it is a supernatural bond. Wives are to obey their husbands as Christ; indeed, her husband becomes a normal pathway to Christ (even if he turns out to be a bad husband and the wife's life a sort of martyrdom in which she loves and serves and prays to save her husband for supernatural motives only). Husbands are to love their wives as Christ loves the

Church and to be solicitous always for their spiritual and material welfare. In this view an unhappy marriage needs primarily a spiritual remedy, compatibility is basically in Christ. In virtually all cases where there is a spiritual union, physical harmony (for the physical is also a real part of marriage, but secondary) follows as a matter of course.

Now in the modern view, in which marriage is regarded as mere mating, sex is primary and the spiritual generally regarded as mere sentiment which is wont to accompany human mating because we are a high type of animal. When marriages go wrong, as they inevitably do where the partners are neither spiritually developed themselves nor conscious of their need for a spiritual union, the modern sex doctor has only one remedy, which is to instruct *ad nauseam* in the art of eroticism. That is why we have so many pseudo-scientific books around on how to make love. When that avenue fails, infidelity and divorce follow, and all their attendant ills.

DR. FREUD

It was really Freud who told the world how to get the most out of being animals. Implicit in his teachings, and very explicit in the teachings of some of his followers, is a quite terrifying concept of what beatitude consists in for the human animal. It is sex, but not ordinary sex such as enjoyed within a circle of domesticity. The Freudians conceive of transcendent sexual experience, a sort of sublime lust. What they have done, in their blind groping about, is to attribute to love at the biological level the honor and the glory and mysticism which belongs to the heights of holiness realized in union with God through supernatural charity. There is only one fitting word for this: it is diabolical.

ORGANIZING THE BARNYARD

It is not enough that we should be reduced to the level of

animals here and there. In order to have a synthesis there needs to be an organizing force, either political or economic. The actual force turns out to be at once political and economic. Socialism is the welding of the two orders. It organizes our economic and daily life down to the last detail, under political auspices. Whichever way we turn we see socialism bearing down upon us. It will destroy the freedom of anyone to resist the animal synthesis.

It is fitting for rational human beings to live in family units, and the natural habitation of the family is the home. Under socialism (of which public housing is the prelude in one respect) family life continues to exist, but in name only. All the old family functions are gone, recreational, educational and religious. Birth control reduces the reproductive function to almost nothing, while impurity and the possibility of divorce destroy the stability of the group. As families fittingly live in homes, so the pseudo-families of socialism live in hives, called apartment projects.

Correspondingly the larger "community" under socialism is not the functional group but the herd, a large mass of people, all alike, gathered together in a subway crush or a baseball stadium or a trade union and acting as one man, or animal.

Socialized medicine is the instrument for consolidating all the veterinarians of the medical profession. When all the doctors are subject to the same discipline, euthanasia, contraception, abortion, human experimentation and psychoanalysis can become universal, prescribed procedures.

Social security, however, is the point of greatest capitulation. We became wards of the state when we exchanged security for freedom, and we gave the state powers which it seems unlikely we shall ever retrieve. The state dispenses all those "charities" which belong to the Church and to the individual Christian. The state provides for us during periods of unemployment, and thereby gains the right to tell us where and when and how to work.

By a natural process too, the state takes over to itself all forms of private enterprise, banking, utilities, shipping, heavy industry and, finally, farming. It looks always as though the state represents the common good, but it never turns out to be that way. The state has a right to regulate banking, farming, etc. It has neither right nor competence to run these, and so it ends up making a prodigious mess of the whole thing.

SUPERMAN

There is a sort of fiction about socialism which is partly true, and that is, that no one governs. The work is seemingly done without intelligence in a perfectly mechanical way. Socialism works through a vast, unwieldy bureaucracy. Thousands upon thousands of men engage in red tape, make studies and reports upon subjects of incredible stupidity, and other thousands file away the reports. The thing finally becomes so complex, unwieldy and unintelligent, that it invites any likely tyrant to cut through the whole confusion and take over. Government by a million bureaucrats easily reduces to government by one enterprising dictator. And what is true on the national scale, by a natural process, extends to global proportions. It is not unlikely that the near future will find the whole world subject to one superman.

Certainly the force and scale of centralization conduce to this state of affairs. Radio, television, jet planes and atomic bombs form the means and the power by which "Superman" can remain in office and operate. All the worst nightmares of the comic strips seem within the possibility of realization.

Not only *could* it happen, but there seems to be a necessity for its happening. That necessity is born of the nature of the synthesis. It is an *animal* synthesis. Rational human beings operate under God, through their intellects and free will. But if we are reduced to animals, our intellects denied the power of real exercise and our wills bound by the absolute conditioning of our lives, then we literally are in need of a guidance above ourselves, some intellect, omnipotent and omniscient, someone who will stand in the position of God to us, to be the sort of God fitting for sub-human animals.

There remains only one question. Who is there so evil and so powerful and so presumptuous as to aspire to becoming this superman, and what would be his purpose in regard to us? When you think of men like Stalin or Hitler you can see that such a man might exist, and even be sufficiently powerful. But these men have always held their power uncertainly, have always been in process of further conquest. Should someone attain to full control he would have to be a Stalin transfigured (in a perverse way). He would have to think himself God and set himself up as God, running the universe for his own glory.

No one except the Devil could aspire to this position, and indeed it is in the nature of the Devil (who is, remember, lord of this world, in a certain sense) to aspire to this absolute authority and autonomy. It must have been he who has twisted us into our present condition, who has brought about the present orientation of society. One speaks of Anti-Christ. Perhaps his time has really come.

THE DEVIL'S STRATEGY

If our superman is to be the Devil, or his henchman, then it becomes clear how he will use us. We exist for God's glory and for the salvation of our souls, which God wills. What would be to the Devil's glory would be the damnation of our souls. We can be certain that he would run the world so as to destroy as many souls as possible.

Now a lot of these things become clear which are just beginning to take form in our society but already suggest their evil end. If the Devil is to bring about our damnation, he must make us commit mortal sin. That is much more important than killing us, and therefore we can expect to be treated nicely in a physical way if it will do us harm spiritually, otherwise not.

Theologians say that there are four root causes of sin: malice, weakness, concupiscence, and ignorance. Only the few sin through premeditated malice, the masses fall through their frailty. It would be to the Devil's tremendous advantage to put us in a position where we were all tempted daily to serious sin. We are already in a pretty bad spot. This is how it works.

In the first place, ignorance of first principles or of any comprehensive Christian knowledge is a tremendous ally of the Devil. When a moral situation arises it is impossible to take a firm stand (as in the case of a public school teacher who teaches the worship of the state because it's slightly disguised and she's not quite certain). Even if the first concession is not formally sinful, the person soon finds himself in a far more compromising position, where the issue is clear but the possibility of retreat cut off.

Or take concupiscence, for we already have that. Adultery comes easier where divorce is legalized. Impurity of thought is almost impossible to resist where obscenity floods the subways, the newsstands and the magazines, when the radio and the office staff circulate dirty jokes, and even Catholic girls dress immodestly.

For anyone who survives these two sources there are other trials. There is the temptation to blackmarketing, born of overindulgence and a stupidly run ration system. There is the temptation to profiteering on rent, born of other men's necessities. But these are only beginnings. What temptations to sin are not inherent in the empty belly of a famine victim or a concentration camp inmate? What a temptation to treachery is presented by torture. What strength is not needed to keep the faith when it is a matter of a job or a ration ticket. And finally, must we all be heroes today, because we may all face the prospect of martyrdom? It looks like it.

·14·

Unless the Lord Build
the House

"WHEN I am weak, then I am strong," said Saint Paul. That must be our constant realization. Our salvation today is in our very weakness, if we turn this weakness into humility. After centuries of being man-centered instead of God-centered, we once more find ourselves up against principalities and powers.

NATURE AND GRACE

It is the old story which we've tried so hard to forget, and which goes way back to original sin.

There is no perfection for us on the human level. Because of original sin we inevitably sink into serious sin. But because of the grace of the redemption we can rise to share God's life. Those are man's only alternatives. What we see in our day is the final havoc wrought by the twofold denial of original sin and redemptive grace, which began with the Renaissance. This denial has even seriously affected Catholics, not only because they participate in a secular civilization, but also because they have forgotten the nature of grace and their need for it.

THE NATURAL DOES NOT LEAD
TO THE SUPERNATURAL

The most frequent error, perhaps, among Catholics is to interpret the phrase "grace perfects nature" as meaning that grace adds an additional perfection to a nature already rectified by natural means. According to this interpretation, a man who had fallen into any of the perverse orientations discussed in this book has not first to pray, but first to act. He must overcome his love of money, find a good job, take some more courses in college or have as many children as God sends, and then he will be a worthy candidate for holiness.

On the contrary, Saint Thomas teaches that grace heals and elevates, that the worse a man's state the more urgent his need of grace. If only he has humility and acts upon it, God will lift him up to the supernatural order and grace will rectify his nature. The naturally good, in this view, seems almost like a by-product of the supernatural, and so it is, in a sense, because it is never an end in itself. If a man's nature is very warped, he simply will be unable to rise at all without divine grace. Alcoholics Anonymous have discovered this profound truth. The theology back of it is that humble prayer wins for us supernatural virtues which fill the natural vacuum, and then build up the corresponding natural virtue. Thus supernatural temperance comes to the aid of the alcoholic and supernatural prudence comes to the aid of all of us who find ourselves in tight spots. Didn't Christ tell His followers not to plan beforehand what they would say when they were brought to trial, because the Holy Ghost would help them?

THE SUFFICIENCY OF GRACE

"My grace is sufficient for you," God told Saint Paul when he protested against his affliction. Again we are told, "Where sin abounds, there grace more abounds." That means that nothing can possibly happen to us which is beyond our (God's) supernatural strength. It is nice to know that in an age where almost anything that threatens to happen is beyond our *natural* strength to endure. In the trial which is upon us humility is the key virtue. Anyone who depends on his own strength is lost. *No one* who asks God's help will be refused and the help will be proportionate to the need. Our God is the God Who in all ages chooses the weak things of this world to confound the wise.

PRINCIPALITIES AND POWERS

It helps to see the diabolical aspect of today's situation, because that is enough to discourage the proudest of us from depending on our own powers. Who are we to pit our feeble brains against an angel?

It is at this point that we should see Our Lady's role. She it is who will overcome the Devil, so we should place all our confidence in her. If she says, "Say the rosary," it might be wise to do so, even if we feel much more like promoting confidence in the United Nations Assembly or interviewing congressmen. We should cultivate the perspective of eternity, in which most of our mad racing around will be seen as pretty minuscule. After all, our late wars have not been very decisive, several world assemblies have been astonishingly ineffectual for the money and talk involved, and hundreds of our great men seem to have fizzled out in a way that makes Saint Francis or Saint Dominic look pretty fine after all. When are we going to give in and do things God's way?

UNLESS THE LORD BUILD THE HOUSE

Once Christians cease to depend on their own natural resources and turn toward Christ, then we begin to see that this is not only a time of great trial but also a time of great opportunity. With Christ all the things which now act to our disadvantage can be transformed into God's instruments and our consequent delight. God, we must remember, always brings good out of evil. If we now have a consummate evil we must be approaching a time of unparalleled good. The Devil may be consolidating the world for the day when we shall all be united in one flock under one shepherd. The diabolical strategy for damning the masses may be the very thing which breaks the curse of their own self-confidence and causes them to cast themselves on God's mercy, by which they will be delivered. The Christian virtue of hope leads us to have confidence in some sort of turning of the tables. But lest it weaken us for the battle to dwell too long on the victory which lies beyond, it is better to concentrate on the need for grace. As the psalmist says:

> *Unless the Lord build the House,*
> *they labor in vain that build it.*